Angels Rescued Us
Father Knows Best
A Child of The King
The Great Physician
His Presence
Love and Compassion
Fish Sandwich
The Power of Prayer
HE IS The Resurrection
God's Timing is Perfect
Where Is Compassion
And The Snow Fell
My Marriage Was Saved
Angels Come In Many Forms
The Faith of My Daughter
Saved By My Mother's Faith
Conviction Comes Before Repentance
God's Word-Promises-God's Presence
Peace Through HIS Protection
Our Challenges Allow Us To Help
His Mercies Are New Every Morning
Jacob's Story
What You Think…You Are
He Sees, He Knows, He Cares
My Journey to Salvation
My Strong Tower
Chaos-vs-Wisdom
Some Through the Fire

IT'S A GOD THING!

'Challenges & Courage For Believers'

Testimonies & Experiences written by:

Hickory Flat Fellowship Church Ladies
and Friends

Compiled and edited by:

Carol McGinnis Yeje

It's A God Thing...

'Challenges & Courage For Believers'

© 2024, Carol McGinnis Yeje,

"All Rights Reserved"

All proceeds go to church funds and ministries of...

HICKORY FLAT FELLOWSHIP CHURCH of God of Prophecy

5301 Hickory Flat Highway [Hwy. 140]

Canton, GA 30115

www.HickoryFlatFellowshipChurch.com

hffellowshipchurch@gmail.com

ISBN: 978-1-304-48889-3

Pictures from Pixabay

Published by:

Carol McGinnis Yeje

P. O. Box 175

Roswell, GA 30077

CAROLMCBOOKS@GMAIL.COM

Contents:

Introduction:			4
Chapter 1:	A Child of the King	[Betty Crowe]	5
Chapter 2:	He Sees, He Knows, He Cares	[Agatha E. Carty Richardson]	8
Chapter 3:	Fish Sandwich	[Evangelist Melody Stephens]	10
Chapter 4:	My Strong Tower	[Church Friend]	12
Chapter 5:	Where Is Compassion	[Evangelist Melody Stephens]	17
Chapter 6:	Saved By My Mother's Faith	[Tammie Powell]	20
Chapter 7:	Angels Come In Many Forms	[Julie Darnell]	25
Chapter 8:	Conviction Comes Before Repentance	[Carol McGinnis Yeje]	27
Chapter 9:	He IS The Resurrection	[Daisylyn Ferris Samuel]	32
Chapter 10:	Love and Compassion	[Evangelist Melody Stephens]	37
Chapter 11:	Our Challenges Allow Us To…	[Laura Davenport]	40
Chapter 12:	The Great Physician	[Carol McGinnis Yeje]	44
Chapter 13:	The Faith Of My Daughter	[Tammie Powell]	48
Chapter 14:	My Marriage Was Saved	[Sharon Layer]	56
Chapter 15:	Chaos-vs-Wisdom	[Evangelist Melody Stephens]	60
Chapter 16:	Angels Rescued Us	[Elora Gilbert James]	62
Chapter 17:	My Journey to Salvation	[Sharon Padgett]	66
Chapter 18:	God Knows—God Cares	[Julie Darnell]	71
Chapter 19:	His Presence	[Lynette Joseph-Ryan]	73
Chapter 20:	And The Snow Fell	[Evangelist Melody Stephens]	78
Chapter 21:	His Mercies Are New Every …	[Agatha E. Carty Richardson]	82
Chapter 22:	Jacob's Story	[Vickie Lawson]	85
Chapter 23:	Father Know's Best	[Carol McGinnis Yeje]	89
Chapter 24:	God's Timing Is Perfect	[Tammie Powell]	92
Chapter 25:	The Power of Prayer	[Julie Darnell]	96
Chapter 26:	Peace Through His Protection	[Sally Sanders Free]	99
Chapter 27:	God's Word-Promises-God's Presence	[Lorna Ferris Joseph]	104
Chapter 28:	Some Through The Fire	[Tammie Powell]	109
Chapter 29:	What You Think…You Are	[Carol McGinnis Yeje]	117

...you say you have received Jesus as Savior...and have no testimony... you are deceived.

A well-known pastor had pastored his church for a year... had a degree in Theology...was known for quoting scripture from memory. The pastor was invited by a fellow college friend, who was also a pastor of a different denomination, to attend a revival at his church. The pastor attended...was 'convicted' [knew in his heart he had not repented & was not truly 'Born Again'--he was raised in church and was taught that 'joining the church' & 'baptism' meant you were Saved]... he went to the altar to pray ...and felt the 'burden of the penalty of sin' lifted as *he received Jesus as his Savior*.

Have you truly repented and know a specific time & place that the 'burden of sin was lifted' when the Holy Spirit came into your heart, and you were forgiven?
If not, don't fail to respond wherever you are, when that 'HEAT LAMP' of conviction goes off in your chest... that's God Drawing you to repentance ...

Pray...repent...Believe...right then...you'll experience the forgiveness and the peace of God's Love ... YOU WILL KNOW that you have passed from 'death' unto 'life' ... John 5:24
Because Jesus died as our supreme sacrifice for sin...
We no longer have to sacrifice animals– I Peter 1:18-19

John 3:3 "Yeshua answered him, "...I tell you, unless one is born from above, he cannot see the kingdom of God."

Introduction:

Our mission is to encourage Believers by reading the amazing examples of 'answered prayer', 'angel encounters', and 'Awesome' Presence of God.

We pray that each person who reads this book, is 'truly Born Again'!

AND...that each reader will examine their hearts to confirm they experienced a 'conversion'...not a 'decision'! And, that each reader will ask their 'loved ones' to give 'their' testimony of Salvation. If they have no testimony, they have no Salvation.

<u>If you have 'no testimony'</u>, [a remembrance of a specific time and place when you repented and you 'felt' the forgiveness of God…and the 'release' of 'guilt'…and the 'Sweet Peace of The Holy Spirit'], then <u>YOU ARE DECEIVED</u>! Don't 'assume' you'll make heaven! Pray again, and 'make sure you know 'JESUS AS LORD'.

YOUR ETERNAL FUTURE DEPENDS ON IT!

Chapter 1

A CHILD OF THE KING!

Written by: BETTY CROWE

5 *And from Jesus Christ the faithful and trustworthy Witness, the Firstborn of the dead [first to be brought back to life] and the Prince (Ruler) of the kings of the earth. To Him Who ever loves us and has once [for all] loosed and freed us from our sins by His own blood,*   Revelation 1:5 -- Amplified Bible, Classic Edition

17 *And if [we are His] children, [then we are His] heirs also: heirs of God and fellow heirs with Christ [sharing His spiritual blessing and inheritance], if indeed we share in His suffering so that we may also share in His glory.*   Romans 8:17 -- Amplified Bible

[Betty was asked to sing at church…and this is the testimony she gave about the song.]

I'M A CHILD OF THE KING

A lady came to church when we had a singing.

She sang, 'I'M A CHILD OF THE KING',
and **GOD MIGHTILY ANOINTED HER.**

It really spoke to me!

Even though I had read and I had been to church all my life.

But, **after hearing that song,** I thought, 'Lord, something's…not all the way I need to be!'

I had been reading and reading stuff…reading the Bible…studying my Sunday School Lessons…**but, when I heard that song I didn't know**—had never heard it before, *it really touched me!*

And, all I knew was **'Praise God…Praise God…I'm A Child of The King'.**

THE LADY TOLD A STORY OF A POOR MAN DIGGING IN A DITCH…

A poor man was digging in a ditch while singing this song.

And, a rich man came along and asked,
*'How can you be singing 'I'm A Child of a King'
while you're digging that ditch?
A child of a king would not be digging a ditch!'*
But the poor man just kept singing, 'I'm A Child of The King'.

I just kept going over all that story in my mind.

One day I was standing at the sink at home, washing dishes. And I was singing…
'Praise God…Praise God…I'm a Child of The King'. The song says, **'His Royal Blood now flows through my veins'!** And I thought, you know, **I've never had a 'blood-transfusion'**—but, **that day, I did!** *I experienced that 'Royal Blood Transfusion'.*

I hope this song touches you.

That Blood that HE Shed on Calvary...He Shed for all of us.

And, I hope…that you know…that you know…that, THAT BLOOD flows through your veins!

Lyrics for 'Child Of The King' – written by: Cindy Walker

VERSE

Once I was clothed in the rags of my sin, Wretched and poor, lost and lonely within,

But with wondrous compassion, the King of all kings, In pity and love, took me under His wings.

CHORUS

Oh, yes, oh yes, I'm a child of the King. His royal blood now flows in my veins,

And I who was wretched and poor now can sing…

Praise God, praise God, I'm a child of the King!

VERSE

Now I'm a child with a Heavenly home. My Holy Father has made me His own

And I'm washed by His blood, and I'm clothed in His love…

And some day I'll sing with the angels above --

---

[3] Jesus answered him, I assure you, most solemnly I tell you, that unless a person is born again (anew, from above), he cannot ever see (know, be acquainted with, and experience) the kingdom of God.
John 3:3 -- Amplified Bible, Classic Edition

[18] For you know that you were not redeemed from your useless [spiritually unproductive] way of life inherited [by tradition] from your forefathers with perishable things like silver and gold, [19] but [you were actually purchased] with precious blood, like that of a [sacrificial] lamb unblemished and spotless, *the priceless blood* of Christ. 1 Peter 1:18-19 -- Amplified Bible

Chapter 2

HE SEES, HE KNOWS, HE RESCUES!

Written by: AGATHA E. CARTY RICHARDSON

Here is a short story about '*the Working Power of God*' and '*His Faithfulness towards us*', His children.

I was diagnosed with heart failure and was asked to see a Heart Failure Specialist Nurse.

After highlighting the "Dos and the Dont's," the nurse mentioned that there was an exercise regimen for anyone with this complaint and that most of its clients benefitted by it.

I agreed and took up the offer.

It was a well-structured regimen scheduled for twelve weeks at two days per week.

Each client had a personal range of what his or her oxygen level should be, **but one of the nurses observed that mine was not keeping within that specific range.**

The doctor was informed about the inconsistency and *ordered a CT scan of my heart with contrast.*
The result showed that I had a blood clot in the appendage of my heart and *needed immediate attention.*
Initially, I had a pacemaker inserted so (with this), things did not look so bright for me at that time.

THE MORAL OF THIS STORY IS:

I was planning to travel from England to the Caribbean for the summer holidays.

Had I taken that trip before the scan, it's not likely that I would be here sharing this story.

God, in His Infinite Mercy, **KNEW** that I needed to be on that role for the exercise classes **in order for the findings to come to light.**

God has been so good to me, *I can't complain.*

I pray that we keep *leaning on the Lord* for Guidance ...

IN EVERY AREA OF OUR LIVES.

Chapter 3

FISH SANDWICH!

Written by: **EVANGELIST MELODY STEPHENS**

_____

Jesus: ¹⁹ *Come*, follow Me, and I will make you fishers of men.

Matthew 4:19 -- The Voice

I know you are probably wondering why this title.

This is a true story, about 'not a typical' Sunday meal.

My husband, David, and I were discussing our meal options. It had gotten later then we had anticipated, so we decided to grab something from McDonalds. *We had just gotten our meal and sat down to eat, when a women approached our table asking for money to buy a fish sandwich. Having no money in my pocket, I offered her an extra burger we had our tray.*

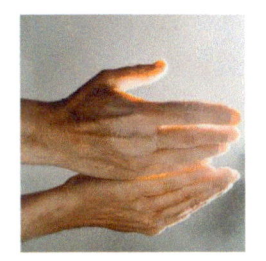

She apologized for asking and explained--

she could only eat very soft food.

In My spirit I knew the Lord had put her in our path.

She journeyed into the restroom and,

I journeyed to the counter –

hoping to find favor with the manager to donate a fish sandwich.

I told him the situation and why it needed to be a fish sandwich.

THANK THE LORD IT WAS SUPPLIED ALONG WITH A DRINK.

She was so very thankful when I handed her the food.

I thought who got the bigger blessing--**ME OR HER?**

See, **WE ARE THE HANDS AND FEET OF JESUS.**

He made us fishers of Men.

May we keep seeking souls whether they are **rich, poor, *dirty*, clean, Man, Woman or Child!**

So--whether it's a fish sandwich or another type of meal,

let the hand of God LEAD you, **and you will be perfectly placed in HIS PLAN!**

Chapter 4

MY STRONG TOWER!

Written by: CHURCH FRIEND

²**He alone is my rock and my salvation,**
My defense *and* MY STRONG TOWER; *I will not be shaken or disheartened.*

Psalm 62:2 -- Amplified Bible

This life I've lived has been a journey!

There have been bumpy roads…with many rocky twists and turns. Life can challenge us to fail, or we can accept those challenges, and choose to prevail.

But My God, upon Him I call…He is there when we fall. He asks only to keep Him close…to carry Him within our very soul!

My Savior, My Lord…He is there with every step! He Walks, at times beside me…sometimes behind me…but, often IN my very steps—for HE Will Carry me when I falter…when I fall.

He furnished Living Water when I was dry…fingers to wipe tears when I cried.

He Chastened and let me stumble when pride and self, marred in. Then, He Wondrously picked me up when I called…and cleansed me once again of it all.

All He Has Ever asked of me is but a moment in the busy times to just acknowledge His Presence and draw nearer to His Side.

To share His Love with others…to acknowledge His Gift of Life…and, the Price He Paid! To remember and remind…the cost was His, so that we may freely abide at His Side.

Author unknown

MY PERSONAL JOURNEY!

There are many times, special moments, and encounters in my life, when God Saved me--- **lifted me on higher ground.**

Each of these were preceded, however, with being [at what seemed] my very lowest. And, at the particular time of each happening or circumstance that I was at my lowest, **"I GREW THRU PAIN"!**

MY SON'S CHALLENGE

One particular time stands out as a total **'God Moment'**...

A friend of our, then 21-year-old, son, nearly overdosed in his upstairs bedroom.

We had always warned and discussed the danger of drugs and ironically believed our young people had listened.

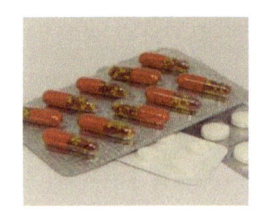

Our son had suffered two severe knee injuries, requiring major surgery...resulting in his losing a scholarship and his ability to play soccer at a high level. The treatment required large [and extended] doses of prescribed pain killers. **RESULTS—**

we had no clue he had become addicted to the pain meds.

The ER Person who came for his friend after the friend's suicide attempt, counseled with us. There were **numerous sessions with counselors**... **discussions of treatment plans**...periods of being straight... followed by relapse...followed by more treatment... and brief respites.

MY DAUGHTER'S CHALLENGE

During the same time period of our son's battle with prescription meds, *our oldest daughter was beginning to struggle with mental issues.* She was diagnosed as being bi-polar.

My daughter was in an abusive marriage, with two small children. **Her husband would prevent her from taking her medication,** *because it cleared her mind, giving her the ability to question his actions---**especially his abusive behavior.***

OUR SPIRITUAL RENEWAL

Both my husband and I were 'surface' Believers, but did not have a true, deep relationship with The Lord.

After several years of ups and downs, I had a complete breakdown.

A very special lady had entered my life as an employee in my business. *She stayed with me...prayed with me...and, directed me in a 'true Spiritual Walk'—* **not just an 'on paper' relationship**—with My Lord.

One night, during this period, I realized **I could no longer bear this burden...fix this mess...and, continue in this state of disfunction.** I started praying. I prayed for hours—**finally**—*I began to feel 'a peace' I'd never felt before.*

**The actual 'Presence of The Lord' was in front of me!
I literally saw and felt 'His Touch'...and...
heard the words—**

'DO NOT FEAR—I HAVE YOU'!

From that day forward, our lives began to change...
MINE—DRASTICALLY!

FAST FORWARD:

My son now has a beautiful family...*is a 'Believer'*...
and, a 'force to be reckoned with', when his children attempt to stray.

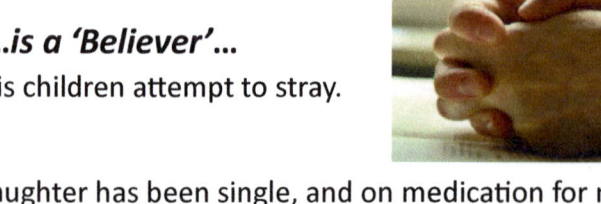

My oldest daughter has been single, and on medication for many years. **She still has struggles, but she knows 'where to take them'!** *Her Faith has lifted her up so many times.*

CONCLUSION:

For each of us,
it is a relationship that *requires...seeks...and, wants more*
OF OUR HEAVENLY FATHER!

HE continues to surprise and amaze...
with 'HIS TIMING'...
'HIS LOVE'...
'HIS STRENGTH'—WITH ALL THAT HE IS!

The more I grow...the more I realize I need to grow!

That period of time, of my greatest challenges, covered 1996 through 2005. As each passed, each year saw positive improvement and spiritual growth in all of us...

and IT CONTINUES TODAY!

Praise MY LORD AND SAVIOR...FOR HIS MERCY AND DELIVERANCE!

Psalm 34:6 - Amplified Bible, Classic Edition

6 This poor man cried, and the Lord heard him, and saved him out of all his troubles.

Jude 25 - Amplified Bible

25 To the only God our Savior, through Jesus Christ our Lord, be Glory, Majesty, Dominion, and Power, before all time and now and forever. Amen!

WHERE IS COMPASSION?

Written by: EVANGELIST MELODY STEPHENS

10 *They have closed their unfeeling heart [to kindness and compassion]; With their mouths they speak proudly and make presumptuous claims.*

Psalm 17:10 - Amplified Bible

Compassion is a simple word.

Definition of compassion is:

Sympathy, Concerned, Sensitive, Mercy, Kindness, Warmth, Tenderness etc...

One day sitting in a restaurant eating a lite lunch.
I began to have a little bit of trouble swallowing.
A small obstruction just enough to irritate my throat.
I began to cough—

nothing bad.

Two women came into this establishment.
Both went to the counter to order.
The Eldest of the two had a surgical mask on – to cover her <u>nose and mouth</u> either for pollen or for sickness that she just did not need.

After ordering, **the younger of the two** [probably in her mid-sixties], **brought the elder lady over to a table of their choosing,** seemly unhappy with my coughing.

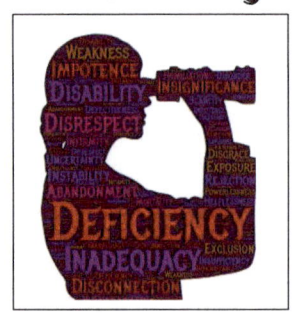

The younger lady said to the eldest,
"I wish she would stop that."

And the other replied,
"Yeah...you want to move?"

Yet...I was not close to them...was covering my mouth--even though I was not sick in body,
they judged.

I sat at my table and prayed for the Lord to let this pass on through.

<u>*My prayer was simple*</u>.

I took a sip of soda—'the Lord answered my request'--I was thankful.

I got up from my seat and put my tray away.

As the elder Lady watched, for I was in her view, **I walked up to their table.**

I asked the Elder Lady, **"How are you today, Ma'am?"**

Very unfriendly, she said, **"Fine!"**

My reply to her was, **"As a matter of fact, I fill great."**

I said as I walked away, **"Have a great day Ladies."**

I walked off knowing I showed them *Love, Kindness, Humanity.*

I was proud the Lord had used me in a situation such as this, after all –

CHRIST HAS, and IS -- COMPASSION.

32 Be kind *and* helpful to one another, tender-hearted **[compassionate, understanding],** ***forgiving one another*** [readily and freely], *just as God in Christ also forgave you.*

Ephesians 4:32 - Amplified Bible

Chapter 6

SAVED by MY MOTHER'S FAITH!

Written by: TAMMIE POWELL

In 1966, **I was 4 years old and a sickly child**.

One day I was at preschool, my teacher Mrs. Snow, had called my mother telling her that I had a fever and that she needed to come and get me.

My mother picked me up and took me directly into the Doctors office.

"Yes", he said, **she has a respiratory infection**, she needs antibiotics and rest.

So off we went to the pharmacy to get my prescription. It had started to lightly sprinkle when we left the Doctors office and now it was raining pretty good.

My mother not wanting me to get chilled out in the rain had instructed me to **"stay put"**, while she went into the pharmacy to get my prescription.

[In 1966 you could leave your kid in the car without getting arrested. It was also a very safe town, and people trusted each other.]

I remember looking out the window at the rain sitting in the driver's seat leaning on the door.
After a few minutes a man pulled up and parked on the right side of our car in the parking lot.

I didn't like the strange man there, and stood up in the car seat to look for my mother. There she was, coming across the parking lot toward me.

I was **SO** *relieved! I had been so frightened!*

But, now, everything was **OK—**

Mom was coming!

As my mother tried to open the door of the car, [an old Chrysler], **the car clicked out of gear!**

The car started to slowly roll forward. It was parked on a gradual incline.

My mother started to panic because she couldn't get the heavy door open.

I had accidentally locked it! *I started crying with my hands on the window opposite of my mothers, as she was franticly trying to stop the car.*

It was not working!

The car was picking up speed, with my mother on the outside yelling at me to open the door! *Hit the brakes!!*

I did both, but the car didn't stop!

I was only 4. I didn't know which pedal to push! **And the door latch was jammed, due to me pulling on the lock latch and my mother's panicked door pulling.**

[In those days, car doors had a button you had to push in, to release the catch--then pull the door open. Not a simple latch like now.]

ALL THE WHILE, THE CAR CONTINUED TO ROLL FORWARD, PICKING UP SPEED.

What I didn't know was that <u>at the end of the slope was a new construction site and it had a giant hole dug for a commercial septic tank and the car was rolling right to it!</u>

My mother running along side--slapped her hands on the hood of the car and yelled, "JESUS PLEASE STOP THIS CAR!", at the top of her lungs.

THE HEAVY CAR STOPPED, ONE FOOT FROM THE EDGE OF THE HOLE!!

My mother just stood there with her hands stretched out over the hood of the car--afraid to move.

Then the man who had parked next to us came running up, white as a sheet,

saying, **"Lady, how did you do that? How did you stop your car?"**

My mother with shaking hands said, **"I DIDN'T, JESUS DID!"**

<u>*Then she opened that stubborn door, reached in, and pulled the emergency brake--*</u>
Then grabbed me! We just sobbed, clinging together.

The man just stood there, removed his hat, scratched his head, put his hat back on, then asked my mother if she was ok?

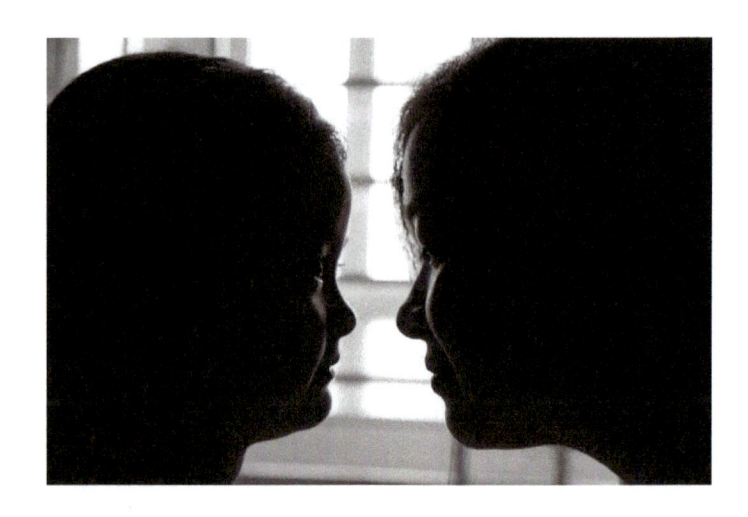

She said, "Yes, thank you! Thanks to Jesus, we are going to be just fine!"

He left scratching his head, mumbling to himself,

"CRAZIEST THING I EVER DID SEE".

After that, we drove home-- PRAISING THE LORD FOR

"Saving me and the Car".

From that time forward -- **Jesus was my hero!**

THE LORD HEARD MY MOTHER'S frantic call AND answered HER panicked prayer.

Chapter 7

ANGELS COME IN MANY FORMS!

Written by: **JULIE DARNELL**

ON ONE OF MY HUSBAND'S NOTORIOUS HOSPITAL STAYS...

...the paranoia and Sundowners sets in, along with coming out of the anesthesia...

...he goes into a Hulk Hogan mode and tries to escape the hospital!

The Nurses rush in, **to try to contain and calm him—**

–as he tears the IV lines in pieces.

No exaggeration here. **PIECES...**

Then...jerks the lanyard off the Nurses neck.

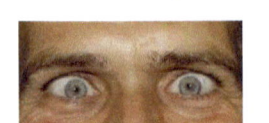

It's a God Thing, that it didn't break her neck.

They could not give him anything to calm or sedate him because they couldn't get close to him without risking, getting hurt.

THIS WAS SO BAD *they called Security to try to restrain him so they could help him.*

Security comes up--two Policemen.

The first one comes in. **It just made him more agitated!**

Then, the second policeman walks in.
My husband looks at him.

He recognized him. *He knew him from when the Policeman was a child.*

He immediately went to my Husband's side and my Husband let him.

He took his hand-- *my husband settled down so much, they could finally give him something to calm him.*

The real God thing in this is that this particular policeman does not work at the hospital.

NO ONE ELSE WAS ABLE TO GET CLOSE TO HIM.

This was third shift. He works with the Sheriff at the Station.

He was there because of an incident that had happened and their were threats against him and the Sheriff put him there to keep him out of them public eye for his safety.

God put him in our path as only God can do.

The circumstances are not a way I would have chosen to see that God works in this situation,

but I'm thankful I did!

. Isaiah 55:8

*For my thoughts are not your thoughts, neither are your **ways** my **ways**, saith the LORD.*

Chapter 8

CONVICTION COMES BEFORE REPENTANCE--
LEAVE THE CHILD ALONE!

Written by: CAROL McGINNIS YEJE

PERSONAL TESTIMONY

I was saved when I was 11 years old.

It was the last day of Bible School at Union Hill Baptist Church in Alpharetta, Georgia. On the last day, it was customary for a visiting preacher to preach a Salvation Message to the older children.

I don't remember anything the preacher said, except the 'invitation'—

"If you don't want to go to hell, won't you come to the altar and ask The Lord to save you?"

Now, I had heard preaching all my childhood. **I had seen many school friends walk the isle and pray to be saved.** And,

<u>I knew I 'should' be saved…</u>

but, somehow, *it never worried me at all.*

[There are many parents that say they don't want their children frightened by a message on 'hell'. But, I can say by experience, that a 'hell-fire' message will never 'scare' or 'bother' them, unless they are under 'conviction'.]

Well, back to my personal experience with The Lord.

In Bible School, when I heard that invitation, **something was different!**
I began to be concerned. I thought to myself… "WELL, I DON'T WANT TO GO TO HELL"!
But it wasn't just a concern in my head or a 'thought-process'.

I felt that 'the inside of my chest was getting very warm'.

And, the longer I stood, the warmer it got—and the more uncomfortable' I became.

28

I didn't know it then, but I know now—I WAS 'UNDER CONVICTION'—
I was being **'drawn'** by The Holy Spirit **to receive Jesus as my Savior.**

And…**for the first time in my life…***I realized 'I' was lost!*

I took one step out into the aisle and
…a few steps toward the altar.
And, **as I suddenly burst into tears,**
I felt as if the **'heaviness'** in my chest just
'blew-out' of my body and the **'worry'** *about going to hell* WAS GONE.
I cried for a few minutes, kneeling at the altar. A friend's mother… (I'll never forget that woman, Mrs. Mansell) …put her arm around me and silently prayed with me.

**I didn't realize the 'change' in me until I opened my eyes.
As I looked around,** *I saw things differently.*

I can't explain it…*but everything 'seemed' different.*

I felt that I was forgiven -- *for 'pitching a fit' when Mama cut my hair;
for making Mama nervous by arguing with my nieces and nephews;* and, mainly,
for making the nice lady, who was my babysitter, cry…
> when I made it clear I didn't want her…
>> I wanted my mama… (I was five at the time).

In short, **anything I had ever done** [in my 11 years], **that I felt was wrong,**
FLASHED BEFORE MY MIND.
And, I had complete peace that I was forgiven.
And, *I didn't even know I felt guilty or 'harbored' guilt* for those things until then.

You see—*I didn't know the scriptures that well. I didn't verbally pray a certain prayer.*
But, **when I said to myself, 'I don't want to go to hell',**

The Lord heard me and 'drew' me by The Holy Spirit.

And as I walked toward the altar, *I was 'saved',* 'BORN AGAIN',
STANDING STRAIGHT UP!

29

NEXT STEPS

And, because I was raised in church, **I knew my next step** ... the next church service, **I JOINED THE CHURCH,** gave my 'testimony' in front of the congregation, and *requested to be baptized*...**AS SCRIPTURE TEACHES.**

[Note: I 'shudder' when I hear a preacher on TV say… 'just pray this simple prayer… *we believe if you prayed that prayer, you got 'Born Again'…* WHAT! He should say, 'If you believe that Jesus is the Son of God; that He died on the cross to pay your sin-debt; and that He was raised from the dead...and you do not know for sure if you died 'right now' that you would go to heaven...and, you feel the 'guilt' of your 'lost' condition...and you know God is calling you to repentance...pray with me—' Then, after the prayer he should say, '...if you prayed that prayer and **felt that God forgave you of your sin,** and ... **...that Jesus came into your heart,** then YOU KNOW IF you were 'Born Again'. Attend a strong Bible-Based Church and talk to the pastor about your experience. He will direct you in your next steps to following Jesus.']

The Bible specifically states **a person must be 'drawn' by The Holy Spirit,** which **'convicts' them** [makes them feel the 'weight of guilt'] **of their sinful condition.**

Then, when they **pray for 'Salvation'**, repenting, and believing that Jesus is the Son of God, the Resurrected Savior, **they will be 'Born Again'.**

A person who **simply prays a short prayer,** *without being 'under conviction'---* even if they've been baptized in every pond *so that every 'tadpole' knows their name--*IS NOT 'BORN AGAIN'.

"The Father loves The Son and has placed everything in His Hands. *Whoever believes in [places his trust in] The Son has eternal life, but whoever rejects The Son will not see life,* for God's Wrath remains on him." John 3:35-36

MAKE SURE YOU HAVE TRULY REPENTED!

After Jesus rose from the dead, He appeared to His Disciples...

"And He said to them, Thus it has been written and is at present on record, that The Christ was to suffer and be raised out from among those who are dead on the 3rd day, and that there is to be preached in His Name, 'repentance', to the putting away of sins—"   Luke 24:46-47 [Wuest]

A person who is 'truly' 'Born Again' may 'stumble', yielding to temptation at times...but **WILL NOT CONTINUE IN SIN**...

"No one who is 'Born of God' will continue to sin, **because God's Seed remains in him;** he cannot go on sinning, ***because he has been 'Born of God'.***"   I John 3:9

So, you see...if you have 'truly' been 'Born Again',

    ...**you first felt 'conviction'**...

            ...**then repentance**...

...**then fully 'trusted' and 'believed on' Jesus as Savior and Lord.**

AND *you know the 'exact' MOMENT you were forgiven—*

[you may not remember the exact date---but you remember the 'exact' place and circumstances--]

AND...OTHERS SHOULD SEE A 'CHANGE' IN YOU.

You will also have a desire to TELL others about your experience, AND, encourage them to pray that God Will Reveal to them their need for a Savior.

13 So brace up your minds; be sober *(circumspect, morally alert)*; set your hope wholly *and* unchangeably on the grace *(divine favor)* that is coming to you when Jesus Christ *(the Messiah) is revealed.*

14 *[Live]* as children of obedience *[to God];* do not conform yourselves to the evil desires *[that governed you]* in your former ignorance *[when you did not know the requirements of the Gospel].*

I Peter 1:13-14 --Amplified Bible, Classic Edition

Chapter 9

HE 'IS' THE RESURRECTION!

Written by: DAISYLYN FERRIS SAMUEL

IT WAS SOMETIME IN DECEMBER OF 2005...

when I started noticing some changes in my body.

I was just feeling tired. My energy level was a bit low, but it was not consistent. I was mostly my usual, energetic self.

I was still actively doing my regular duties and feeling fine **except for the occasional (bout of) tiredness.**

DURING THIS PERIOD, I was also preparing meals for my two nieces (Veron and Lynette) who were pregnant with their first babies and were having a tough time with their pregnancies.

I also was having regular bible reading and prayer with them as well as their babies in utero.

THIS WAS A JOY TO DO!

ON FRIDAY, 16TH JUNE, 2006...

I had my annual medical checkup. All was well! On Saturday, 17th June, I started my monthly (menstrual) cycle. On Sunday, 18th June (which was Father's Day), the flow became heavier. On Monday, 19th June, all hell broke loose. *I started bleeding nonstop.* On Tuesday, 20th June, 2006, after my husband, my family and I concluded that this was more than my cycle, *I decided to go to the emergency room.*

MY HUSBAND PRAYED FOR ME BEFORE WE LEFT.

Even though I was still bleeding, after prayer I noticed it was at a slower rate.

That day (June 20th), **I was hospitalized (in Antigua) and diagnosed with Leukemia.**

I was forty-eight years old.

Upon admission to the hospital, my blood count was 6.7 and I was still losing blood. **I spent seven days in the hospital in Antigua.** After seeking God for direction, *He gave specific instructions* to travel on June 26th, 2006 for further medical attention.

After I informed my family and doctors of this date, my family started the process of securing an air ambulance to San Juan, Puerto Rico. They also started talking with the doctors in Puerto Rico. The doctors needed me to travel right away and advised my family to get me on a commercial flight and forget about the air ambulance. The doctors further advised that it was very risking to travel on a commercial flight, but they needed me there to start working with me.

I was airlifted to San Juan, Puerto Rico.

I know I was taking a big chance, **but I was in God's hands.**

I landed safely along with my sisters Yvonne and Lorna.

WHEN I ARRIVED IN PUERTO RICO...

I was admitted to Hospital Universitario Centro Medico (Central Medical University Hospital).

I was diagnosed with Acute Myelogenous Leukemia FAB Classification M3.

According to my diagnosis I was very critical. I was near death.

My white blood cells count was over One Hundred Thousand and my red blood cell was at 10.1. I had to be treated with very **aggressive chemotherapy** because of the aggressiveness of the Leukemia.

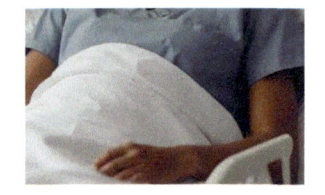

It was a very rough journey during my hospitalization. *I had swollen hands and feet, mouth sores etc.* **You name it – I had it.** This was something I did not have any knowledge about, so *I asked my sister Yvonne (a registered nurse) to be responsible for the medical aspect.*

My sister Lorna was always the "go to person," so she dealt with everything else that we needed. I spent Thirty-Two days in the Central Medical University Hospital and was discharged on July 28th 2006.

AFTER MY DISCHARGE, I RETURNED HOME TO ANTIGUA..

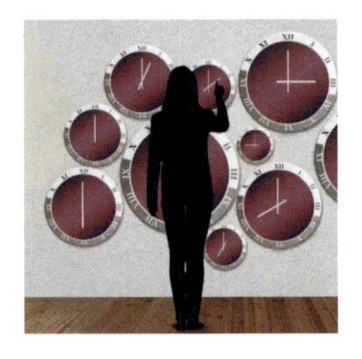

but had to continue treatment both oral and intravenous chemotherapy for the next three months as part of my discharge plan. During this period,

I had to travel back and forth, between Antigua and Puerto Rico for treatment. Then I had to make **yearly trips for Twelve (12) consecutive years.**

This was extremely costly. We watched our finances dwindled away.
We truly had to live by faith, but we saw God as our Jehovah Jireh through it all.

BATTLING LEUKEMIA AND GOING THROUGH THE TREATMENT WERE EXTREMELY CHALLENGING TIMES.

<u>I lost all my hair</u>. **It came off all at once one day.**
> I was able to lift it off like a wig since it was braided.

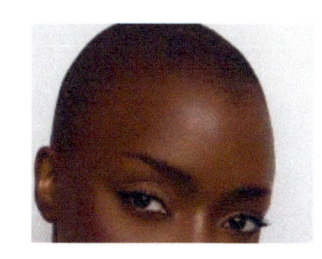

My feet were swollen on occasions, there were times when I was a bit confused, lost appetite for some foods, could not tolerate the smell of certain fragrances etc. ***There were also times I could not carry my pocket book because my hands and arms were painful from taking the chemo.***

ANOTHER CHALLENGE WAS THE ISOLATION.

My association with family and friends was very limited because of the seriousness of my condition. **Beside doctors' visits both in Antigua and Puerto Rico, <u>I had to be indoors for the next Three years because my immune system was very low.</u>** *My husband, Eugene was appointed as pastor for less than a year when I came under this attack. As his wife and a minister, I was not able to assist with the work for Three years, since I could not attend church services either. In spite of this isolation,*

my Lord drew me into another level of worship and communion with Him.

THERE IS SO MUCH MORE THAT I CAN SHARE.   This is just a portion of my journey.

I can say to God be all the glory! He is Healer, Deliverer, Provider, and Protector.

<u>He is the one who resurrected me from death to life</u>. **Great things He has done!**

I glorify the King of Kings and the Lord of Lords. HE IS AWESOME!

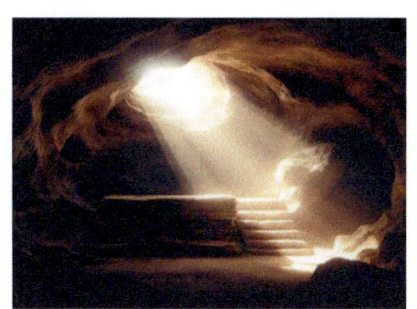

FURTHER EXORTATION & INSTRUCTION REGARDING THE SPIRITUAL ASPECT

In 2004, **God told me to separate myself unto him. He also directed me to go on daily prayer walks.** Mondays were my lock-in days with God when **I prayed, fasted and read the word of God**, along with a **few books on prayer and fasting and warfare prayers**.

It was during this time of separation, that I came under this terrible attack in my body. I believe that the season of separation unto God prepared me for what was coming.

After I received the doctor's report (the diagnosis of Leukemia) hospitalized in Puerto Rico, I was moved in my spirit to send specific instructions regarding the approach to prayer on my behalf. First, I told my sister Yvonne (who is a registered nurse) that her responsibility was to deal with the medical aspect, while I dealt with the spiritual. After the medical team gave her the report, **I passed it on to the intercessors to have them pray.** Next, **I told my family, my friends, my prayer partners/ intercessors, and our Mountain Movers Prayer Group how to pray about this attack**. I instructed them to call it out by name because it has a name. **My brother, Bishop Ferris was the District Bishop of the Church Of God Of Prophecy in Antigua at the time of my diagnosis. I also sent messages to him to ask the church to worship in prayer and praise concerning my condition when they gathered for the fellowship service that Sunday afternoon.** ((My sister Lorna's role was to write all my instructions since my hands and arms were mostly swollen while hospitalized in Puerto Rico).).

The scriptures I stood on during my journey were – **Psalm 118:17 and Isaiah 53:5** *because these were the scriptures the Holy Spirit gave me.*

Psalm 118:17 [KJV]

"I shall not die, but live, and declare the works of the LORD."

Isaiah 53:5 [KJV]

"But he was wounded for our transgressions, he was bruised for our iniquities: the chastisement of our peace was upon him; and with his stripes we are healed."

<u>TO GOD BE ALL THE GLORY FOR GREAT THINGS HE HAS DONE!</u>

God did a wonderful thing! Heaven rules...!

Chapter 10

LOVE AND COMPASSION!

Written by: EVANGELIST MELODY STEPHENS

Psalm 68:19 -- Amplified Bible, Classic Edition

¹⁹ Blessed be the Lord, Who bears our burdens and carries us day by day, even the God Who is our salvation! Selah

I started out my day as planned.

I had several things to do that morning.

One thing on my list was to *go to the post Office and mail my letter*.
Call me "Old School"—

**I like to go inside and hand my mail
to the Postal Worker at the counter,
instead of putting it in the mail box.**

Ahead of me was a Lady that was crying and telling the Postal Workers *she was sorry for being "Scattered Brain"*. As I handed my mail to my friend, the Postal Worker,

I silently said a prayer for the Lady.

I turned to exit the building and she came out behind me trying to hold it together. As we walked down the sidewalk, she started telling me her hurt and how her life changed so quickly.

We stood together on the sidewalk talking and, Wow--How the Lord worked!

Her son had been Tragically Killed in a car accident in another state where he lived.

She was now waiting for his body to arrive here from out of state for a funeral and burial.

She told me how he had gotten his life cleaned up from drugs and alcohol and had accepted Jesus as His Lord and Savior.

She said, **"I have accepted Jesus too!"** And I proclaimed, **"Me Too!"**

As I ministered to her, **I reminded her that one day we would be reunited with our loved ones that passed on before us.**

She revealed that this was no ordinary day…
that **his passing was on his 25ᵗʰ birthday** and
HE WAS HER ONLY CHILD.

On this day I was aggravated with myself because I wanted to be at the Post Office earlier then I was--**but God had ordained this day and meeting with her.**

As I stood on that sidewalk with her arms around my neck crying,

I OPENLY HAD PRAYER FOR THIS GRIEVING MOTHER.

When I finished praying, she said, "Jesus put you here for me!"
With tears streaming down my face I said,
"Yes he did! He did it for both of us."
She asked me if I was a Minister. I said, "Yes ma'am I am."

Once again, she said, "Jesus did this for me!

He put you right here at this time when, I needed to have --

LOVE AND COMPASSION,

and encouraging words of prayer!"

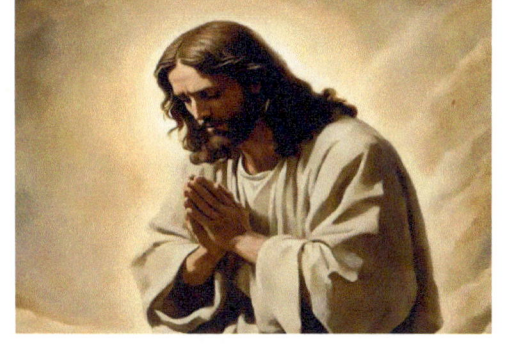

I told this new sister in the faith where I go to Church. **I invited her to come and join us.**

Amazingly, turns out **she knew right where we are located.**

So, I hope to see her here in Church and, also, look forward to seeing her in Heaven!

When I got into my car,

I just sat there and cried and told the Lord I was sorry that I was aggravated.

<u>I THANKED HIM FOR DELAYING ME SO MY STEPS WOULD BE ORDERED OF HIM.</u>

Chapter 11

OUR CHALLENGES ALLOW US TO HELP ENCOURAGE OTHERS THROUGH THEIRS!

Written by: LAURA DAVENPORT

1 Thessalonians 5:11 -- Amplified Bible, Classic Edition

[11] Therefore encourage (admonish, exhort) *one another and edify* (strengthen and build up) *one another, just as you are doing.*

I have had many times in my life where I know God has walked closely with me.

If it were not for His saving Grace and presence, I never would have made it through.

DEATH BY SUICIDE

After being saved through Christ at the age of 7 years old, I went through many years of ridicule and teasing from others: not because of my beliefs, but because of Satan's control on others.

My first major trial was my sister's death.

She committed suicide when she was 24 and I was 19.
After a very volatile home life and many disappointments,
Beverly could not take it anymore.

While she professed to be Christian--and many will say how could she do that if she was Christian--she had not had the opportunity to mature as a Christian to the point where she could rely on him, solely. This event served to strengthen my belief.

I only had Him to believe in--Him to run to in my grief.

If that was the purpose of my sister's death, then I needed to grasp it and be aware of the sacrifice.

ANSWERED PRAYER FOR OUR HEARTS' DESIRES

Many years later, after getting married, **my husband and I went through the trials of infertility.**
I cried many tears yearning to be a mother.
GOD led us through the church to the answer and **for that I am grateful.**

I now have **two beautiful adult daughters** that God sent us through being faithful to his word and believing-- *He had the answer to our longing.*

SUDDEN DEATH OF THE HEART

In January 2017, my sweet husband left me to be with the Lord.

We had been out of town for the New Year and had just gotten back. After two days of pain which we thought was related to an elbow injury he has a few months before, he went to the hospital. There **he found out** that **he had a heart attack that had destroyed the center section of his heart.**
He was life-flighted to another hospital, intubated and put on heart bypass before I got there.
After multiple surgeries and procedures, **HE PASSED AWAY 10 DAYS LATER.**

I never got to hear his voice again after leaving the first hospital.

God has walked with me every step of the way.

From having to finish raising my two teenage daughters, getting them through college and helping them through their grief, **to facing my own grief and learning to manage a household alone.**

God has never left me.

I cry out to Him sometimes and he holds my hand.

He soothes my inner turmoil.

I am able to take the next step forward because I know he is there to catch me if I fall.

ONLY THROUGH HIM HAVE I BEEN ABLE TO MOVE FORWARD.

HEALTH JOURNEY

About 3 years ago I began to lose my hearing.

After many tests it was discovered that I had a condition called **Pseudotumor Cerebrii**. Basically, **it is elevated pressure in the brain.**

The elevated pressure had caused --
damage to my hearing, balance, vision and caused horrific headaches.

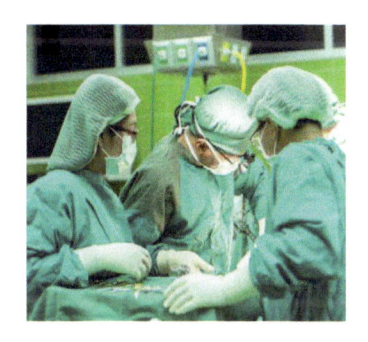

It was determined that I would have to have a **ventriculoperitoneal shunt** that runs from the brain to the abdomen to drain off excess spinal fluid. I had that **shunt** placed and **within 6 months had to have it changed 3 times** due to getting clogged. *One time I lost vision in my left eye as I was driving.* **The Good Lord got me home without killing myself or anyone else but it was not easy.**

THE BLESSING I HAVE RECEIVED THROUGH ALL OF THIS IS THAT I CAN SUPPORT PEOPLE GOING THROUGH SOME OF THE SAME THINGS.

Whether it is **suicide, infertility, grief or illness,**
GOD HAS EQUIPPED ME TO HELP PEOPLE BECOME OVERCOMERS.

Only through God's wisdom and love are we able to survive the trials of this life.
God has recently placed a woman going through diagnosis and treatment of Pseudotumor Cerebrii in my path to coach and to lead in prayer.
    Coincidence? I think not. She had grown away from church.
Perhaps hearing how I have overcome my challenges, and, me helping her overcome hers, **will bring her back to a reliance on God.**

Chapter 12

THE GREAT PHYSICIAN!

Written by: CAROL McGINNIS YEJE

GOD'S HEALING POWER HAS NEVER BEEN QUESTIONED BY ME.

I believe we should all have annual physicals by our doctors, and, go to the doctor when we have health issues that rest and Tylenol will not cure.

However…**we should all pray for healing!**

Sometimes, the healing comes **after** the doctor appointment, as we heed the medical knowledge of our physicians.

BUT WAIT! Sometimes, **the healing comes**, and **we know**

it's not because of the earthly doctor's diagnosis and treatment.

Sometimes, THE GREAT PHYSICIAN **chooses to heal us**—*no medicine—no surgery—*

—no long-term recovery **is necessary!**

That's what I experienced…and I want to share that experience with you.

I enjoy writing books…especially children's books…with pictures of animals.

My friend takes the pictures used in most of my children's books. When I begin creating my story for a specific book, **I could possible review over a thousand photos,** as I decide which one is the perfect shot for a specific page in the book.

This selection process *takes hours,* **with my right hand on the 'mouse',**

as I continually 'search and click'.op[

I noticed **my right hand began to feel 'stiff'**, and, **daily, was becoming more painful,** as I worked on my book. After the pain began, **in a few months' time,** *it had gotten so bad, I could not hold anything in my fingers*… **and the pain was so great,**

I would have to elevate my hand on a pillow in the bed at night.

Finally, I realized, I needed to go to the doctor… **praying all that time, for healing.**

My first appointment, the doctor said 'severe carpal tunnel'.

[Carpal tunnel syndrome (CTS) is a common condition that occurs when the median nerve in the wrist is compressed.]

He also scheduled an expensive **'nerve test' for both hands**, *since the left hand was having the same symptoms.*

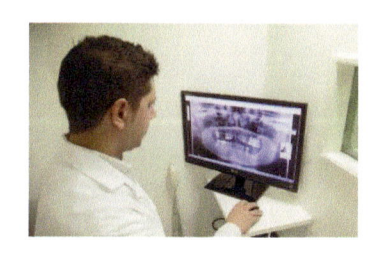

After the results of the 'nerve test',
I was referred to a 'hand surgeon' for a possible operation on both hands.

45

NOW...ON TO THE 'HAND SURGEON'.

As I sat across from him, with a small table between us, he said, **"OK...let me examine your hands."**

I raised my hand from my lap, and gestured toward him, but, *when he touched it, I jerked it back in pain.* ***I couldn't stand for my right hand, especially, to be touched...by anything!***

He said, *"You have 'pseudo-gout'! I cannot perform surgery, until the gout is cleared up."*
[Pseudogout is a form of arthritis characterized by sudden, painful swelling in one or more of the joints.]

So...**the 'hand-surgeon' sent me to an 'arthritis specialist'!**

NOW...ON TO THE 'ARTHRITIS SPECIALIST'.

After an exam...blood test...and meds, the arthritis doctor sent me home.

Well, *I could only take the meds for 2 days*...they helped, but, were too strong for my stomach.

Now...**continuing to pray**...

Ask God for What You Need

⁷ "·Ask [Keep asking], and ·God will give [it will be given; the passive verb implies God as subject] to you. ·Search [Seek; Keep seeking], and you will find. ·Knock [Keep knocking], and the door will open for you." Matthew 7:7 -- Expanded Bible

⁵ While he was at Gibeon, the LORD appeared to him in a dream during the night. God said, "Ask for whatever you want me to give you." 1 Kings 3:5 -- Expanded Bible

⁴ He asked you for life, and you gave it to him, ·so his years go on and on [length of days forever and ever]. Psalm 21:4 -- Expanded Bible

⁸ Don't be like them, because your Father knows the things you need before you ask him.
Matthew 6:8 -- Expanded Bible

¹⁹ "·Also [Again], I tell you that if two of you on earth agree about something ·and pray for it [for which you have asked], it will be done for you by my Father in heaven.
Matthew 18:19 -- Expanded Bible

¹³ I truly believe I will see the LORD's goodness ·during my life [in the land of the living].
Psalm 27:13 -- Expanded Bible

¹³ Then to the centurion Jesus said, Go; it shall be done for you as you have believed. And the servant boy was restored to health at that very moment.   Matthew 8:13 – Amp. Bible, Classic Ed.

…and trying to determine what diet is best for severe arthritis patients…

within 2 weeks…I WAS HEALED!

To give you a 'glimpse' of how 'miraculous' this healing was…

HERE'S WHAT HAPPENED NEXT.

I have 'cervical disc disease' in my neck. God has helped me 'maintain' relatively normal activities by carrying a cushion to put behind my back when seated. I had an incident that caused my neck to begin to bother me, so, I made an appointment with the doctor.

This was the same doctor that did the nerve test, and referred me to the 'hand surgeon'.

When the doctor entered the exam room, the first thing he asked was, **"Well, let's take a look at your wrists."**

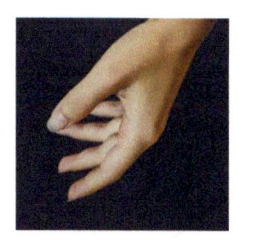

I handed him my hands, and he turned them over to see my wrists.

He looked as if he had seen a ghost! He said, **"You didn't have surgery?"**

I said, **"No, sir."** He said,

"But, I saw how serious your hands were…especially your right hand!"

I said, "I know…it's just amazing…they just got better!"

He said, **"That IS amazing!"**

I said, **"Well…I AM A PRAYING WOMAN!"**

THEN--TOTAL SILENCE…

as God 'pricked his heart' reminding him of WHO the actual healer, IS!

Chapter 13

THE FAITH OF MY DAUGHTER

Written by: TAMMIE POWELL

In 1992, I was helping one of my three daughters, Breanna, out of the bath tub, when she winced as I steadied her with both hands, one on each shoulder.

"**Ouch mommy, that hurts.**" It was a gentle touch, so I leaned back with both hands one on each shoulder and compared them. **Her right arm bicep was swollen.**

My mind went directly to her constant hours on the playground, playing "tether ball". It was her favorite.

As I buffed her dry and wrapped her in the large towel, I talked to her about maybe leaving that game alone for a while, giving her arm a rest and playing something else.

"**Okay mama**", she agreed. "**All better now.**"

I didn't think a lot about it until the next day.

She bumped her right arm on the door knob-- *tears came to her eyes--* she grabbed her arm and just stood there-- *breathing deep.*

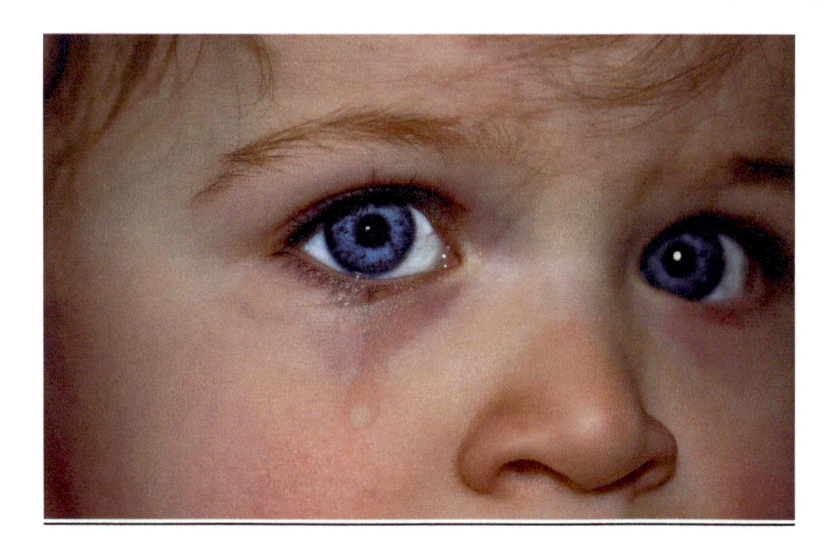

Breanna was not a crier, nor was she a complainer.

NOW SHE HAD MY COMPLETE ATTENTION.

I dropped to my knees and gently massaged her arm--feeling for something-- looking for a reason why her arm was hurting so much from such a gentle bump.

THEN I FELT IT- *a hard knot in her right bicep.*

My husband did the same when he came home that evening.

Holding Breanna on his lap, he gently massaged her arm.

His face became set and blank, showing no emotion.

He knew that something was terribly wrong. He very casually cuddled our daughter and called his brother whom he worked with, telling him that he would not be at work tomorrow because we were taking Breanna to the Doctors office in the morning and he needed to be there. All the while watching my face over her little curl capped head.

My heart dropped. After we tucked our girls in bed we had a long talk. **He didn't want to assume the worst but**…*we both knew it wasn't good.*

We prayed, "Please Lord Jesus, whatever this is, please save our little girl, keep her safe, touch her with your healing hands."

Now, I want you to remember that this is 1992, there are no cell phones, no internet, no instant way to look things up. So, we waited until morning and was at the door to the Doctors office when they opened.

The Doctor was a young man and took us right in.

He sat Breanna on an exam table --chatting with us and her -- keeping it light and cheerful, while he examined her arm.

X-rays were required. Then we waited for them to be read by the technician.

When the doctor came out of the room where they look at the Xrays, *he didn't look at us!* Instead, he went directly to the Doctor's office.

The mood in the office changed from light and cheerful, to dread!

No one made eye contact--*everyone stopped talking.*

When the Doctor finally called us in to his office, you could hear a pin drop. And when he opened his door, I about jumped out of my skin--completely tense.

Of course, we had prayed the night before, **and** that morning as we were driving--but at that moment,

I WAS NUMB!

I didn't have the presence of mind to call out to the Lord.

I was shutting down with fear.

As we went in to his office, he suggested that Breanna should,

"stay out in the waiting room, while us grown-ups have a talk".

Breanna looked up at us with wide beseeching eyes, shaking her head no, curls bouncing everywhere.

A calm came over me. I looked at my husband and said,

"No. We are open and honest with our children. It's her body we are discussing. I think she should be present."

The Doctor looked so disappointed with me, but said, *"Alright lady."*

As we went in I realized it was his personal office and that there was only two chairs for us. So, I lifted Breanna into my lap. **He looked at us with a sad and heavy face and said**,

"I think she has Osteosarcoma, a rare cancer of the bones mostly found in children."

Then he took a deep breath and said,

"Right now, the only cure is to hope it's only in her arm and to amputate it.

If it has spread, I'm not sure there is a treatment that I can suggest."

Breanna, sitting in my lap, started shaking. *I put my arms around her and drew her into me instinctively shielding her, trying not to cry.* The Doctor offered us tissue and paused for us to absorb all the information that he had just unloaded on us.

Breanna twisted around and said,

"Are they going to cut my arm off mommy?"

I said, *"No one's doing anything right now, we are just talking about how to get you better."*
My eyes met my husband's, over the top of her head--**overwhelmed and reeling.**

Breanna twisted around in my lap and said, *"It's okay mommy.*

Jesus just told me that I am not getting my arm cut off and to not worry."

We looked down and said, *"Ok, well that works for us!"*

We were thinking—*'out of the mouths of babes'!*

We were shaky, teary and clinging to that hope!

The Doctor had a surprised look on his face. **He shook his head and said,**

"*I only know of two Doctors in the United States*, west of the Rockies that actually treat this and …**you're not going to believe this**… but *one is here in this area visiting* and I went to a conference last week and heard him speak. *I have contacted his offices and are still waiting for a reply.* **Do you want me to make an appointment for Breanna to see him?** He is at UC Davis Medical Center downtown Sacramento."

Two days later we were in Sacramento California, a three hour drive from our home in north California. We were there to see the specialist Joe Matthews, who by God's grace was visiting our area and teaching at the Medical University.

Breanna's doctor had told us that *Dr. Matthews was choosing a few cases to follow while he taught on her particular cancer.* **Maybe, just maybe, he would choose her.**

So…*we prayed, that God's Will be done,*
should he choose to, **PLEASE SPARE OUR DAUGHTER.**

We wanted a miracle! We wanted complete healing! But, if the Lord had another plan, please prepare us and help us get through this, whatever happened.

As we waited in the exam room, *Breanna stood there clinging to a pink bunny* that had been given to her by our little church the day before.

Then a brown-haired middle aged man walked in--picked up Breanna--sat her on the exam table--grabbed a stool and dropped it to her eye level, and said,

"Hi I'm Joe", who are you?"

She gave him the biggest smile, and said, *"Silly, I'm the patient."*

He smiled back and leaned in and said, *"Well 'patient', I don't do amputations."*

She leaned in to him and **nearly touched his forehead with hers—**

POKED HIM IN THE CHEST WITH HER LITTLE FINGER and said,
"Good--because Jesus said no one is cutting off my arm!"

He threw back his head and laughed openly. **Then he asked Breanna to be his client**, not the other way around—*we expected to be begging for her to be his patient.*

53

WE LIVED AT UC DAVIS MEDICAL CENTER FOR TWO YEARS.

Breanna's chemotherapy treatments were extreme. *She was very sick!* We were at the medical center 4 days out of every week--coming home for 3 days then back again--provided her blood counts were good enough to come home. *I slept by her side in a reclining chair those days.*

Many things happened! *Many blessings that kept us from despair.*

THE LORD WAS ALWAYS WITH US!

AFTER 2 1/2 YEARS, *Breanna was told that she was in remission and she did not need chemotherapy anymore.* The staff at the hospital fell in love with our little girl--she never complained--she never cried--she was always sweet. So much so that the hospital administrator approached us asking if our little family would *please be a model for their hospital color book*, it was to be their first, and they would like to name it--

"BREANNA AND BUNNY GOES TO THE HOSPITAL."

They wanted to take pictures of Breanna in various positions in the hospital like, *Breanna & Bunny get their blood drawn*, *Breanna & Bunny get an MRI,* etc..

Because of the different kinds of chemo that Breanna had been given, there was a concern for extreme side effects. They told us that she would have eyesight problems. That's ok-- **She wears contacts now, and sometimes eyeglasses, they work just fine.**

They told her she might not be able to have children.
She has 2 full grown sons, smart and both beautiful with no birth defects.
They told her that she might not be able to use her arm--that it might just be a dead arm.
It's not! She uses it just fine.

If you didn't know her you would never know that she once had cancer.
THEY TOLD HER THAT SHE HAD A 30% CHANCE OF SURVIVAL--
less, **if they didn't amputate her arm.** *But here she is, grown to a beautiful woman now.*

They never amputated her arm! **They didn't need to!**

God was in control and HE always keeps His Word.

The Lord *did answer our prayers*, just *not in the time line we were hoping for.*

54

<u>God Used Breanna</u> *to share her hospital room with other children,* **who listened to her story.** *All of the children's family members that visited them,* **heard her story.**

Our town who loved her, still loves her and **knows her story.**

She was 'Blessed' **to have met the nurses at the hospital, who would stay late and come in early, asking for the shift that would be taking care of Breanna.**

She was 'Blessed' to have met the 5 Doctors doing their internships with the University Hospital that were following Breanna's care.

One of the doctors was doing his thesis on Breanna's case. **He marveled at what Breanna had endured, with grace and dignity.** *He wrote about Breanna's faith and the faith of her family, and how 'faith' impacts thoughts of well-being and hope with healing.*

They may not have known why they all wanted to spend time in our room, but we did. **They could feel the touch of God–it draws us, like moths to the flame.**

WE CAN'T HELP BUT CRAVE IT--<u>OUR MAKER'S TOUCH.</u>

*He does answer prayers--***ALL OF THEM**–*just sometimes, not the way we may expect it.*

Chapter 14

MY MARRIAGE WAS SAVED!

Written by: SHARON LAYER

Ephesians 3:16 -- Amplified Bible

16 *May He grant you out of the riches of His glory, to be strengthened and spiritually energized with power through His Spirit in your inner self, [indwelling your innermost being and personality].*

Ephesians 3:16, encourages me that my *inner being or soul* can be strong with power according to Christ's riches.

<u>HIS POWER IS LIMITLESS!</u>

So *why do our prayers lack confidence?* **The answers often surprise us?**

This was me years ago, as I complained to God about my *agonizing* marriage!

In fact, as I prayed, I actually made a **list of ten things that needed to happen** for me to stay in my marriage.

Specifically, I listed **actions that my husband needed to take** or

I was packing up and calling it quits!

I was **self righteous**, heartbroken, ANGRY, **WRONGED**, and *determined,* as I wrote that list.

I think *the list was really* <u>my excuse to leave</u> <u>with a chance to blame it all on him</u>.

Imagine my surprise, when one day, **in the midst of our silent six weeks of anger,** *my spouse began to speak*...

There I sat, **fuming**, in the passenger seat next to him, thinking,

"How dare you talk to me, after all you've done?"

He began with, **"You know, I've been thinking about us?**

I really think that I should"…

and he proceeded to name the first thing on my list!

He then named *every single item on my list*,

IN ORDER,

one through ten, almost word for word.

I NOW know, there is limitless power in our prayers,

especially when pouring out our whole heart of emotions to God.

I'll tell you, **THAT DAY**, I was in the floorboard, unseen tears flowing inside, because I knew that I had revealed my list to no one!

God's Holy Spirit power put that list into my husband's loving heart because *Jesus knew His power was needed* **to soften my angry, hurting heart that had given up completely.**

My answered prayer gave me hope, faith, and strength in my husband and in my God, who saw me in my despair.

It had saved my marriage!

So, how has my imperfect marriage survived for over forty years, now? It is through many, sometimes daily, answered prayers. Maybe, not all of them were as specific or seen as clearly as that list, **but every one was through the limitless power of an absolutely trustworthy, loving God.**

So, *whatever you are praying for*, A MARRIAGE OR CHILD OR SICKNESS,

pray -- **KNOWING that YOUR PRAYERS HAVE POWER,** and

expect Him to answer them with His power !

Chapter 15

CHAOS – vs – WISDOM

Written by: **EVANGELIST MELODY STEPHENS**

Wondering why Graduation Bulletins?

Are we not in the season of little ones graduating –

Pre-K, High Schoolers --**getting their diplomas,**

Or, College Students -- **receiving their degrees?**

I have watched my Niece for the past four years juggle home life, College exams, her parents and Grandparents being called home to be with the Lord. So, a lot of emotions had filled her to the point she would say,

"Ok Lord you have to help me".

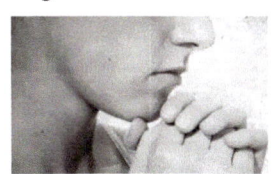

Last week I had the honor of watching my Niece graduate from the University of West Georgia. I was a proud Aunt sitting in this beautiful Coliseum.

My heart filled with a lot of emotions: *sadness, happy, joyful, etc…*

When it came her time to receive her diploma, **we cheered and clapped,** and suddenly it got quiet as I simply said out loud, "Thank you Jesus"!

It appeared as if surround sound was on—**it was loud!**
The place erupted with Claps and laughter.
I was giving God the Glory!

Shortly after, **Satan tried to enter and disrupt the ceremony.**

A fight broke and a couple of people were injured in the stands.

Police quickly moved in, arrested and escorted the person out of the building.

See--Chaos tried to invade but Wisdom overshadowed.

In (Proverbs 10:11-12) *"…the mouth of a righteous man is a well of life: but violence covers the mouth of the wicked. Hatred stirs up strife: but love covers all sins."*

So let us as Christians, graduate daily in Christ,

as our minds gain knowledge, and our souls prosper.

Chapter 16

ANGELS RESCUED US!

Written by: ELORA GILBERT JAMES

FROM 'PRAISE' TO 'PRAISE'

On Saturday, 26th of October, 2024, my husband (Dwane) and I <u>attended the 24th annual World Creole Music Festival, in Dominica.</u>

Now, my husband enjoys hearing the artist <u>Kassav</u> and the French bands. Although I do not favor that genre of music, *it was still quality time spent together enjoying something he loves.*

We spent all night at the festival. The next morning (even though there were still more artists remaining in the lineup), we left at about 6 a.m. after he heard his favorites. As soon as we got to our vehicle, I took off my jacket, hopped in, and then Dwane drove off.

Our drive home from town usually takes over an hour, but I had to have been very exhausted because <u>I fell asleep in a flash.</u>

<u>**About quarter of the way home the unexpected happened.**</u>

Still deep in sleep as my husband drove home, I heard a voice saying,
"I need you to hold on to something—
as tight as you can and do not let go."

All of a sudden, *<u>I felt that my body I had risen up,</u>* but did not fall back down into my seat.

Awakened and startled, but with my eyes still shut,

<u>I held on tightly as the vehicle kept moving and flipping in the air.</u>
(I would soon find out we had gotten into an accident).
Once the vehicle landed and I finally opened my eyes, I realized that my right hand was wrapped around the headrest of the driver's seat.

Surprisingly, **I found myself precisely seated in the driver's seat and hugging it tightly.**

<u>*Why am I in the driver's seat?*</u>
<u>*Where is my husband?*</u>

I looked over to the passenger side and noticed the windscreen was broken up. Looking around, <u>I saw blood everywhere</u>. There were so many things going through my mind at this time. <u>Overcome by this scene and consumed by my thoughts, I started to panic.</u>

Frantically, I began to call for my husband.

"Dwane, Babe, Dwane, Babe! <u>***Where are you?***</u>"

I KEPT ON CALLING.

"I am here," Dwane eventually shouted!
<u>What a relief it was when I finally heard his voice!</u>

Immediately he made his way towards me and opened the driver's door. <u>He was covered in blood.</u> Seeing my husband all bloody I began panicking again. "Where exactly did you get hurt?", I asked him.

<u>He reassured me that it was only some cuts on his hand and he was okay.</u>

As I exited the vehicle, **I was happy and extremely thankful that we were both alive.**

Then, for a moment, overwhelmed with emotions at the thought that we could have died and left our young daughters,

I began to cry.

<u>*While the tears flowed,*</u> I busied myself by ensuring that my husband was really okay.

<u>At this instant, many questions flooded my mind:</u>

"Babe, what really happened? <u>How did you end up outside of the vehicle?</u> How did I land on your seat?
<u>*I asked one after the other*</u>.

Of course, <u>he could not explain any of it,</u> but proceeded to share what he experienced that morning.

At first (when we started for home), **Dwane intended to tell me that he needed to pull over to sleep for a while.** However, <u>he dozed off before he could do so.</u>

<u>*In the fraction of time that he fell asleep at the wheel my husband shared*</u> that he also heard a voice.

This voice said, "Wake up boy...you are driving, wake up."

<u>The moment he opened his eyes</u>, *he realized he was going to hit a culvert.*
As he swerved to try to avoid it,
<u>the passenger's side took the hit then the vehicle went flying, flipping as it went</u>.
At that point, **he remembered being outside of our vehicle airborne.** Right then,
<u>he had made up his mind that his life was over</u>.

He thought he would land on his head and break his neck from his trajectory, <u>*but God had other plans*</u>. Instead, **he landed flat on his back**. While lying there, he looked up and saw the vehicle—*with me in it*—coming down towards him.

He believed that it would have landed on him and crushed him - <u>*but God*</u>...

This time **(seeing death)** <u>*Dwane literally gave up,*</u> talked to God, closed his eyes, and **passed out for a little while.** As he was coming to, <u>*he heard my voice calling his name*</u>. That was when he slowly moved from behind our vehicle **(not from under it)** <u>*to open the driver's door for me.*</u> Even though both his head and face were swollen, **Dwane was in one piece**.

Praise the Lord!

AFTER THIS ORDEAL, WE WENT TO THE HOSPITAL—

We got examined and had some x-rays taken. Although we had bumps, cuts and bruises, and of course aches and pains, **the x-rays showed that we were both fine**.

We were dumbfounded, but *totally indebted to God*.

Now, weeks after our accident we have replayed the details quite often.

My husband still cannot say when the driver's door was opened.

How do we explain that the only thing that was ripped opened, was the driver's door?

Dwane believes that **his angel** ripped his door opened to **take him out of the vehicle to put me in his seat,** thus, *securing me from the impact and possibly very serious injuries.*

And how do you explain that a plus size woman (me) **was safely repositioned from my passenger seat to his driver's seat sitting hugging it?**

There are still many unanswered questions, but we believe that on Sunday, the 27th of October *God sent His angels to take care of us.*

Who would have thought that soon after an evening of creole music and great company, that the journey home would have overshadowed our date night?

All things considered, our supernatural rescue by God's angels far outshines all that occurred.

THANK YOU LORD!

We are miraculously alive to tell our story of such a terrifying experience!

Amazed at all that occurred, we are both forever thankful...*forever grateful*!

GOD IS ABSOLUTELY AMAZING!

"For He shall give His angels charge over you, to keep you in all your ways. In their hands they shall bear you up, lest you dash your foot against a stone." Psalms 91:11-12 (NKJV)

"The angel of the LORD encamps all around those who fear Him, and delivers them." Psalm 34:7 (NKJV)

Chapter 17

MY JOURNEY TO SALVATION

Written by: SHARON PADGETT

John 3:3 -- Amplified Bible

[3] Jesus answered him,
"I assure you and most solemnly say to you, unless a person is born again [reborn from above—spiritually transformed, renewed, sanctified], he cannot [ever] see and experience the kingdom of God."

I have been in church my whole life, even before I was born. **My Mom always went to church** and my father went part of the time, until I was five years old and then-- *Praise The Lord--* **he was saved during the spring revival.** After that, he hardly missed a Sunday or Wednesday night service.

When I was eight on a Saturday night, *I* **decided** *I wanted to be saved* so I went and told my parents I felt like I needed to be saved. They talked to me a few minutes, and then we bowed down in the living room and **I went through the motions** but *I never really asked Jesus into my heart.*

Well, then a couple of weeks later **after joining the church,** *I was baptized!* And for several years *I thought everything was alright* -- but along about the time I was 13, *I started having doubts* and **I knew in my heart I hadn't been saved – but my pride** kept me from telling anyone that I thought I wasn't saved.

This went on for years—

I became a Sunday School teacher,

a youth leader,

Church pianist

and **held several more positions in the church,**

but I still wasn't saved.

Oh, *I knew how to talk the talk,* but **I sure didn't have the walk –**

and this went on for many years.

About the time I was 50, God started working on me, many, many nights –

I would lay in bed and think if Jesus comes back tonight I'm going straight to hell.

I would pray and try to talk to God but I know my prayers were going no further than the ceiling -- *this went for another couple of years.*

During this time I became a grandmother--Riley was born. One day when he was two, I was babysitting him, I had to go to the restroom and I told him to stay right there in the living room, that I would be right back.

I wasn't gone but a couple of minutes but when I came back into the living room, **Riley wasn't there**. I just figured he had gone in one of the other rooms so I started looking and calling his name--but **I couldn't find him**.

I searched the whole house, every room, every closet -- I even checked the outside doors, but they were still locked.

My heart was racing, where could he be.

Then it hit me –

the rapture had taken place and I wasn't going.

At this point I was standing in our bedroom--I fell on the bed weeping and begging God to please give me another chance -- when about that time

I heard Riley start laughing in the living room.

I ran in there and **there he stood in the exact spot he was** when I had gone to the rest room, holding the same toy just **looking at me smiling**.

I grabbed him, hugging and kissing him and thanking God that he gave me another chance.

I know some people think he had to be some where in the house and I just didn't see him. But, I searched every room and closet anywhere he could be and he wasn't there. I was even screaming his name and he never answered me! TRUST ME--HE WASN'T THERE. **I don't know where he was but I know God used this to show me** *I wasn't saved.*

As soon as Kim came and picked him up and they left –

I hit my knees and started praying asking the Lord to save me --

And, **right then and there is when I was saved at the age old 52.**

Now I know beyond any doubt I am SAVED! Praise The Lord!

So-- **if anyone is doubting your salvation please don't let pride**

or anything else stand in your way.

You must not miss the opportunity to really be saved.

Chapter 18

GOD KNOWS! GOD CARES!

Written by: JULIE DARNELL

I really think God used my husband...
To show me, first-hand, how 'his' hand is in everything.

My Husband was short of breath and feeling tired.

With a history of heart problems, his doctor wanted to do a heart cath. He had him go to a heart interventionist. [My Husband has had heart caths before, with other doctors.]

<u>They did the Cath and were to put in stents, if necessary.</u>

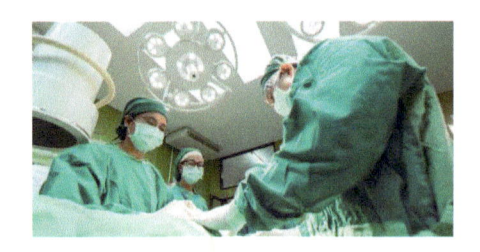

This particular doctor starts to do heart Cath and comes out right before he starts and says,

"I want to do a CT on his lungs, since he is short of breath, to make sure it's not his lungs".

<u>After the scan, the doctor said his lungs are fine</u>...

BUT...

<u>he has a large nodule on his thyroid that needs to be removed.</u>

We go to the surgeon.
  They remove the nodule.
<u>It's stage 3 thyroid cancer</u>!

As shocking as this news was to us...

<u>we were thankful the doctor now knew how to proceed.</u>

<u>HAD HE NOT DONE THE CT, THE CANCER PROBABLY WOULDN'T HAVE BEEN FOUND.</u>

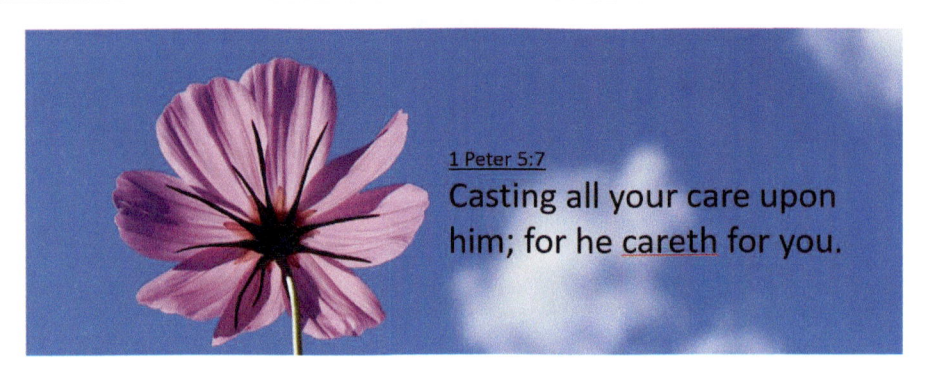

1 Peter 5:7
Casting all your care upon him; for he <u>careth</u> for you.

Chapter 19

HIS PRESENCE!

Written by: LYNETTE JOSEPH-RYAN

EARLY ENCOUNTERS OF HIS PRESENCE

During my very early adolescent years (in the 1980s), I was very active in our youth group.

When **I was about <u>twelve years old</u>, I was given an assignment to preach a sermonette to the congregation.** <u>I had preached before at my local church.</u>

Then again, maybe I should say exhorted not preached, but now this was a district service since it was **International Youth Week.** *I humbly accepted the assignment as I always wanted to do my part in God's service. Being more of an introvert, I was not feeling settled to stand before a larger congregation of seven local churches gathered together.*

Considering that I usually go to prayer and fasting about things, I decided that would be my move. As I reflect on two Bible characters **Daniel and Jehoshaphat** and **how they addressed their matter,** <u>I set my face to seek the Lord concerning this matter</u>.

One day, while lying prostrate on my bedroom floor in prayer and fasting, I heard my bedroom door opened. I listened carefully to hear my mother's voice, but instead I heard two footsteps.

I FELT AN AWESOME PRESENCE FILLED MY ROOM, and *then I heard His Voice.*

The Lord said, "Daughter, daughter, do not speak with excellence of word, but with simplicity so that the youngest child can understand."

I WANTED TO TURN TO SEE HIM, BUT COULD NOT MOVE.

I was awestruck!

I continued basking in His presence in reverence and thanksgiving for His instructions.

This encounter and the instructions from God ...

...gave me confidence to present my sermonette to the larger congregation.

The Sound of His Voice gave me the assurance that He **WILL** be with me always. From that day, *I knew it was not about my weaknesses or personality traits*, but what God **WANTS** me to do and to whom **He sends me.** As His Servant,

I am on Divine assignment and He is with me.

THANK YOU LORD FOR YOUR ABIDING PRESENCE!

"…and lo, I am with you always [remaining with you perpetually—regardless of circumstance, and on every occasion], even to the end of the age." Matthew 28:20b (AMP)

"My sheep hear my voice, and I know them, and they follow me." John 10:27 (ESV)

BEFORE MIGRATING TO THE UNITED STATES OF AMERICA,
I was a civil servant and worked at the airport, in Antigua.

It was early one morning in October 2002. My night shift ended, but it was raining so **I decided to sit in the office and wait it out**. Watching the clock, I realized I had to leave very soon in time **to get the car home for my father** to head out to work. Thank God, **the rain ended** approximately 7am! Immediately, **I got up and left the office to head home.**

When going on the road, I usually pray a road prayer asking God for protection.

I did not park in the employees' parking lot where I could use the elevator downstairs. I parked in the visitors' parking lot. This meant **I had to walk up the corridor to use the wet stairs** down to the first floor then to the parking lot. **As I turned and neared the top of the stairs**,

I heard a voice say, *"Hold on to the rails."*

There wasn't anyone behind me.

Without thinking, **I immediately obeyed.** I stood at the top of the stairs, switched my bags and thermos to my left arm and hand, and then coiled my right arm around the rail starting with an over, under, over action. **With my arm and hand securely placed, I put my right foot forward to take my first step.**

Immediately, like a lightning bolt,

I shot off from the top of the stairs directly to the bottom in one flash, going straight through the cleaner's legs, and **hit the wall behind her.** The cleaner (pushing the rainwater off the steps) in amazement of my rocket-speed descent, shouted,

"Oh God Oh God!"

She helped me gather up my stuff then asked,
 "Are you alright?"
In total shock, all I could do was nod a, **"yes."**
Regaining my composure I slowly stood up, took my stuff from her, retrieved my slippers and in soaked jeans **headed to my car.**

THE TRAUMATIC INJURIES I SUSTAINED THAT DAY TO MY BACK, TAILBONE (COCCYX), LIGAMENTS, ETC., STILL AFFECT ME.

What happened in a flash changed my life forever.

Today, *I still use a custom-made coccyx pillow to sit on and continue in pain daily.*

I know that voice was The Holy Spirit instructing me to hold on to the rails. Interestingly though, was the unusual way I held the rails – <u>a coiled arm instead of just simply holding</u> the top with my hand. <u>My coiled arm delayed my release from the rail which in turn prevented me from banging my head on the wet, tiled-concrete stairs</u>.

I know beyond a shadow of a doubt that was solely **The Holy Spirit** *guiding my arm because I would have just held it the usual way.*

It is so amazing that **my head never reached the steps**. God held me up! To this day, *I believe my obedience to His voice and His guidance saved me from something more tragic...*death.

The weapon that formed against me did not succeed!

GLORY TO GOD!

He has proven to be *My Refuge and My Present Help* in trouble.
I am here today because of God's protection! *Thank you Lord!*

"No weapon that is formed against you will succeed;" Isaiah 54:17 (AMP)

"God is our refuge and strength [mighty and impenetrable], a very present *and* well-proved help in trouble." Psalm 46:1 (AMP)

My childhood quest was to "know" God.

I had a hunger and thirst for God and His kingdom.

This was developed into a lifestyle of **prayer and fasting**, reading and meditating on God's word, **prayer walks—** <u>through the woods and along the beach</u>, *praise and worship, etc.*

Even when I had a new baby and was not able to fast because I was nursing him, <u>I was intentional in setting aside quiet times to maintain this lifestyle.</u>

The quietness of night worked perfectly for me.

My routine was to stay up late at night down through the wee hours of the morning.

I would then join our morning prayer line.

MY DESIRE WAS TO PURSUE GOD FOR AN ENCOUNTER.

One morning in 2012 while on the prayer line, during worship and prayer,
I came in contact with the Fire of God – THE HOLY SPIRIT.

I began to experience an intense heat –
a burning that started to move extremely slowly from my feet to my head and in like manner back down to my feet. This was **all day, every day** and **continued for almost a week**. During this time, *my left ear was on fire. It was burning too, but my right ear was fine.*

THIS WAS A NEW AND STRANGE EXPERIENCE...

...but I basked in it with thanksgiving, while asking God to consume me.

Yet, *I was wondering what it meant.*

<u>*I eventually shared my experience with our intercessors.*</u>

During our conversations, they shared, in essence, <u>*that God was drawing me and setting me to hear His voice*</u>.

A later conversation with the prayer line leader led to another revelation.

<u>*He shared that he saw a calling to a ministry of healing on my life.*</u>

This surprised me, but over the years I prayed and waited patiently for it to be fulfilled. *This was realized in the birthing and journey of our intercessory prayer ministry namely*

Encounter With The Holy Ministries.

Over the years, **this ministry has opened new avenues for more encounters as we make intercession and worship God nightly.** <u>FILL ME UP LORD!</u> **My quest continues!** It is for a lifetime. <u>*Thank You Lord for Your Overwhelming Presence!*</u>

"But seek first the kingdom of God and His righteousness, and all these things shall be added to you."

Matthew 6:33 (NKJV)

"Blessed are those who hunger and thirst for righteousness, for they shall be filled." Matthew 5:6 (NKJV)

Chapter 20

AND THE SNOW FELL!

Written by: EVANGELIST MELODY STEPHENS

It was not a typical winter's day in February.

I was out walking in my back yard along with my puppy "Chance".
I was dressed <u>*unseasonably*</u> in shorts, tee shirt and flip flops.

I was surely in my happy place.

I have two fish ponds in my backyard.
Typically, the ponds are frozen over during this time of year,
and, if you know anything about fish ponds--
the fish do not eat in the wintertime.

<u>**But not this year because it was 74 degrees outside.**</u>

Sounds comical, doesn't it? As I stood there feeding my fish, I thought how much I liked this warm weather even in February—but, you know, I would like to see some snow before winter ends. I simply looked up at the sky and here is what I prayed for:

"Lord, you know everything about me and you know I love this warm weather even in February, but Father I want to see some "Snow"! Lord, you hold every season in the palm of your hands in Jesus' Name I pray--Amen."

Doesn't scripture say in John 16:23, 'whatever you ask in my name'?

Well--I asked—and, yes, **I did receive!**

Saturday, February 8, 2020, SNOW--YES PRETTY SNOW.

I was excited to see this wonderful event take place!
In fact, I wept knowing what I had prayed for was now falling
basically, just a few days after I prayed.
*My Heavenly Father heard a simply prayer and
with childlike faith I held on that I would see snow.*

Standing on my back deck and Chance,

exploring his 1st snow. I was all excited as well,

I lifted my hands with tear dimmed eyes and said, *"thank you Father, it's beautiful".*

Somewhere in our sub-division an angelic voice exclaimed, *"Hey everybody, It's snowing!"*

Quickly I replied, "It sure is sweetie--and isn't it beautiful?"

As time progressed on--WOW--we were completely white.

A PICTURE OF BEAUTY!

Is it not amazing how God holds everything in the palm of his hand?

My husband, David, was recording this snow event and as we watched it fall, *the flakes at times were huge almost like feathers*—and, at times, *they seemed to get small*. The thing about this event <u>**how the Lord takes all of our prayers**</u> -- whether they are huge or they may seem small, *they all are important to Him and he wants to hear from his children.*

The next day being Sunday we were able to have church. *All of us were talking about the snow* and each were telling *how much they had gotten* and how *some had traveled* from out of town *where the snow was really great in measure.*

In fact, I had told **how I prayed for snow just a few days before** -- and how happy I was that I had dressed in "summer apparel", but not winter apparel -- and *I explained how fish do not eat in the winter and how great they enjoyed being fed.*

My brother in the Lord said, **"You mean because of you it snowed?**

YOU REALLY PRAYED FOR SNOW?"

And with a big smile I said, **"Yes, Brother Myron, I wanted to see snow and I also said aren't you glad to know that I can pray and get answers to prayer?"**

As Christian, do we not want to see the Lord answer our prayers?

Don't we need to be confident when we ask individuals to pray for us
whether it is for a healing or a financial situation or greater yet salvation.

My hopes are to have confidence in 'God's Power to Answer'--*from a small prayer such as simple as a snow fall, to someone that needs a prayer that is life altering.*

JUST REMEMBER WE ARE CHILDREN OF THE HIGHEST GOD

and *HE CARES ABOUT EVERY ASPECT OF OUR LIVES!*
After all, **he created us**!

In fact, scripture says in Jeremiah 1:5:
"I knew you before you were even formed in your mother's womb."

So, does not that tell us all... He wants to hear from us and be in our everyday lives?

So, *as easily as the snow fell--* put all things in the hands of the Lord.

ANSWERS WILL COME TO ALL OUR PRAYERS.

Chapter 21

HIS MERCIES ARE NEW EVERY MORNING!

Written by: AGATHA E. CARTY RICHARDSON

IN 1960 I MIGRATED TO ENGLAND.

I WAS ONLY SEVENTEEN YEARS OLD..

I pursued a profession in nursing and became a **Senior Registered Nurse**. Over the years, as a senior nurse, occasionally I had to work night duty. One morning after finishing a night shift, one of my colleagues said to me,

"Agatha, **the word for today is**,
> *whatever comes your way give thanks to God.*"

I went on to say,
> "**If I live**, *I would be very happy*...
>
> and **if I die**, *I would also be very happy*."
>
> Then I started to sing, "*Que Sera, Sera*...**Whatever will be, will be**..."

I left the office, got into my car…

…switched on a (cassette) tape which said,

"If you never needed the Lord before, you sure do need Him now."

It was a dark and cloudy morning with rain showering down. I drove to a cross road which had a reflector light about thirty yards away on my left.

I was there looking right and left to be sure when I could drive out.

At one instance, *I looked right then left and thought everything was clear,* **but no sooner as I drove out** *a large Volvo Station Wagon came at high speed and hit me on my right side.*

Within that moment, I felt everything inside me turned over and it appeared as if I was on a chariot with horses going round and round in circles.

When I came to myself…
…I noticed my car was smashed to bits
and *was a total right off.* **My shoes were off my feet**
and **I struggled to exit via the passenger's side.**

I thought I'd better be quick before the car blew up with me inside.

I hurried out as fast as possible with my bare feet.

Where I had to walk was covered in prickles, but miraculously none pricked me.

I held on to my side and kept saying-- **"Thank You Lord!"** *(Remember the word for today)?*

However, the Lord sent an angel in the form of a lady…

…who asked me if I would like her to phone anyone for me.

She informed me that she already called the ambulance and it is on its way.

I GAVE HER THE NUMBER OF THE NURSING HOME WHERE I WORKED THAT NIGHT AND ALSO MY DAUGHTER'S TELEPHONE NUMBER.

Then I asked her for her name and telephone number because I wanted to thank her for the kindness she bestowed on me. Surprisingly... she did not give me neither name nor number.

She simply said 'it's ok' and disappeared.

All I can say is that, **at that moment**, Psalms 91:11-13 **was fulfilled in my life.**

11 – *"He shall give His angels charge over thee, to keep thee in all thy ways."*
12 – *"They shall bear thee up in their hands, lest thou dash thy foot against a stone."*
13 – *"Thou shalt thread upon the lion and adder: the young lion and the dragon shalt thou trample under foot."*

Thankfully, no injuries were found when I arrived at the hospital.

All the staff kept asking if I was experiencing pain.
I had no pain for the whole day, *but the next morning*
my side was like the colours of the rainbow.
That was the only evidence that a car hit me on my side.

If one needed assurance and proof of how deep the Father's Love is, here is another example:

The same morning of my accident, my son was on a trip away in Tenerife. When my family contacted him and *gave him the news of my accident*, he was standing in a shop buying me a gift. Interestingly, *he was holding a brooch marked "guardian angel."* Hearing that news my son began to shake and held the brooch tightly. In astonishment he shouted, "What is this!" Then slowly he tried to regain his composure.

ISN'T OUR GOD WONDERFUL?

I've always asked Him, "Please don't let me leave behind an unfinished task."
He absolutely honoured my prayer, because one year later ...

...my husband (Neil) completely lost his sight.
That would have been the unfinished task if I was taken away that morning.
I was my husband's nurse for ten years.
Then the Lord called him away four years and eleven months to date.

THANK YOU LORD FOR ANSWERED PRAYERS!

Chapter 22

JACOB'S STORY!

Written by: VICKIE LAWSON

MOTHERHOOD WAS SOMETHING I HAD ALWAYS DREAMED OF…

…for as long as I could remember. *I always loved playing with babies even as a child.*

However, when I became an adult and got married and after several years, we realized we could not conceive.

I was heartbroken… but then began to realize **God had another plan** and we began looking into adoption.

We did not care about the race or nationality of the baby, *we just wanted to be a mama and a daddy.*

Adoption is not cheap or easy, so we began to look into foreign adoption, thinking our chances would be better for a fast and cheaper adoption.

While we were doing our research someone approached me about a **local private adoption** and the baby would be due in August of 1987. However, *it was not meant to be* and us and our families *were very disappointed*.

We still continued to pursue other avenues.

I had worked with a special friend, Virginia, for several years and she knew my story.
Exactly 2 weeks before Christmas in 1987, I received a phone call that
changed my life forever!

Virginia called and asked if would be interested in a 2-month-old baby boy.

Of course, we were very excited.

Virginia explained she went to pick up her daughter from the babysitter and **they asked her if she knew anyone who like to adopt this baby boy.** The husband and wife explained to her that **this was his sister's baby** and she originally planned to give him up when he was born but changed her mind when she held him. **She had several problems and did not take care of him. He ended up in the hospital with pneumonia.**

When his uncle found out he agreed to bring him home…

…but knew they could not physically or financially give him what he needed.

This couple had already adopted 1 child in the family with special needs along with their own children. They were also in their 40's at this time.

They had been praying God would send the right family.

Virginia immediately gave us all the contact information…
...*and the journey to adoption began.*

After many conversations the birth mother agreed to sign over her rights and surrender this precious boy into our care. We finally had everything worked out and on December 23, 1987,

we picked up our bundle of joy.

Virginia, interestingly enough, **lived in the city of Bethlehem** and we went to her home next and she had gotten us many items we needed.

So, we always say Jacob was

OUR BABY FROM BETHLEHEM AT CHRISTMAS.

We began our journey home that evening to *surprise our families*. We made the decision not say anything to them prior to this since they were so disappointed when the first one fell through.

We arrived at my husband's family and just walked in carrying our little boy. They asked whose baby we were watching and we said ours. They called the family members and they began to come and celebrate with us.

The next part of our journey was to surprise…
… my mom and dad.

We arrived and as soon **as mom saw Jacob, she knew…** and the hugging and crying began. *All my family came…*

…and a lot of the neighbors who had been praying for us.

Christmas of 1987 was the best ever!

Everyone was out buying things for him as we didn't have very much. We took Jacob and had his picture made with Santa, which was very special to us, **we were now a family**.

Adoption is a process and after the mother signed the papers...

...she still had 10 days to change her mind. Some people worried and asked us if we we're concerned, **but I always answered and said NO**, because...

...I knew God had placed Jacob in our family to stay.

The time came when the 10-day period was over and we were all very excited.

We had to find an attorney to do all the paperwork and go through the court system. We found a great one and began the process but we hit a little snag as the birth father had not surrendered his rights. The attorney had his name and city and was not able to locate him so we had to keep waiting.

April of 1988 our attorney found out he had a brain tumor and of course had to take time off. So we are still waiting and I asked his secretary if she would give me the name of the birth father and the city *so I could try to find him.*

She gave me the information and **I began to pray that God would lead me in the right direction**. This city had many, many listings with that last name but not the first name.

I made a decision that I would pray and start calling these listings. When I picked the phone book, I chose a number with a lady's name, and **I know God led me there**. I called, and a lady answered and I asked if [giving her the birth-father's name] was there and she said hold on. *He came to the phone and I began to tell him who I was and why I was calling.* **I gave him the birth-mother's name** and **asked if he would sign over his rights to Jacob.**

He immediately said yes and signed a week later.

The journey continued...*as this was May of 1988...* everything was finalized February of 1989. **I never doubted this was the child God had placed with us.** However, *to continue to show you the power of God,* when all was said and done our attorney only charged us 500 dollars.

In the 80's, it was into the thousands of dollars and we didn't even know how we would pay for the adoption.

God was in the control of all of the process *from beginning to end* **and**

He showed His power in a mighty way.

Jacob is now a man and has a child of his own.

I am so blessed to be his mom and a grandmother to his daughter.

GOD IS GREAT!

Chapter 23

FATHER KNOWS BEST!

Written by: CAROL McGINNIS YEJE

MY MOTHER WAS THE 'ROCK' OF OUR FAMILY!

In 1977, **she had a stroke.** She had always worried about having one, **since her father had died in his 50's from a stroke.**

Mama had 6 children, and 7 grandsons, and 4 granddaughters.

Several of them had children of their own…so,
        the 'greats' were coming!
Over her 67 years, she had dealt with many
        heartaches and challenges.
But, she always 'survived' and 'thrived'…
        and was the 'queen of hearts' to all of us.

We knew Mama was at risk within 6-8 weeks prior to her stroke,

because **she had 'phlebitis' in one of her legs…with blood clots all over**…every ½ inch or so in any direction. The doctor said, *if just one clot gets loose and hits her brain, she would have a stroke.*

She had been confined to bed or recliner for all that time.

On the day of her stroke, **I just happened to call my grandmother** [who lived with mama], and asked to speak to mama. Grandma became upset and said, **"Your dad had to call an ambulance.**
She threw up a lot of blood…just filled the sink!"

Panicked, I began calling my sisters and brother.

Memories of the next few days of her gradual fall, into a comma, and eventual death, are too painful to relive.

My message I wish to share, is **the 'tenderness of God'**, and

        'His Amazing Grace',

during our time of saying goodbye to our precious, Saintly, mother.

Mama had been in the hospital for 4 days.

Her last day, **my 2 older sisters had left the hospital to get a motel room together**, near the hospital. **My other sister and I were together with her in the hospital room.**

She could no longer communicate…

and **had labored breathing** [the nurse had inserted a plastic 'funnel' into her mouth and throat to help her breathe].

I looked at my sister and said, "Let's pray over her!"

WE WENT TO HER BED-ONE ON EACH SIDE-AND JOINED HANDS OVER HER.

I don't remember everything I said in my prayer...*but through my tears*...

I remember saying, "Heavenly Father…please don't take her from us… **we love her so much!"**

Almost immediately, God Spoke to me! *He said,* "I…LOVE…HER…MORE!"

Then, I knew, mama was 'going home'!

After the funeral, **I was amazed at the 'joy' I felt!**

It was as if my feet were 'tethered' to the ground…

and, **if someone would just 'cut the cord'**, I would float up in the air, and join her!

Through this experience, **I had a 'new awakening' of God's Love for us.**

We MUST NOT question God's Will! HE can be 'trusted'!

Many Christians get angry or begin questioning God's Will, if their prayer is not answered, THEIR WAY! But, days after confirmed, **OUR FATHER KNEW BEST!**

The undertaker told us that mama had cancer spread 'all over her body'. **She was suffering in silence**…Six months later, my brother died from lung cancer at age, 48. Then, many family tragedies and deaths. **My point**…mama, who loved her family more than herself and would die for any of them, **never had to go through ANY disappointments, disgrace, heartbreak or loss**, because --- 'GOD LOVED HER MORE', and took her home.

Mama was a praying woman, and displayed love in every word and action. My dedication to 'making her proud' includes…**living for Jesus as Lord…loving my family unconditionally…and, looking for opportunities to do all I can, personally and prayerfully, to bring ALL of her family to heaven.** *She has 28 great-grands, 56 great-greats, and 3 great-great-greats.*

I humbly request that you remember 'MAMAW'S BUNCH' in your prayers.

As a songwriter, I am best known for '**I WANT US TO BE TOGETHER IN HEAVEN**'.

After mama died. I wrote. '**MY HEART IS WHERE MY HOME IS**'!

This is the chorus:

Since Jesus Saved my soul…I knew heaven would be my home,

'Til Mama died, my heart was here below,

But now my heart is where my home is, and I'm homesick,

I love the Lord, and I'm longing for home.

[You can listen to any of my songs on my music channels— www.youtube.com/@togetherinheaven – www.rumble.com/togetherinheaven -- also, Spotify, Pandora, ITunes, Amazon, Apple, etc.]

Chapter 24

GOD'S TIMING IS PERFECT!

Written by: TAMMIE POWELL

Once when I was a young woman, *I threw back my head and simply asked the Lord,*

"Please! Can I just--for one day--have my house, and yard clean, and all the laundry done!"

I was tired and exasperated!

I had worked all day on my home...cleaning, washing and cooking for my husband and 3 beautiful, but very **ENERGETIC** daughters.

The day before I had tackled the laundry in the morning and spent the rest of the day in our yard--falling into bed after dinner time. So... *I was feeling sorry for myself.*

That morning, as I sipped my coffee and gazed out the window, *my husband's dog, "Bambino"*, a 110 pound Rottweiler, *was digging In my not-so-perfect flower bed--*as our oldest daughter ran by *with one of my clean white sheets from the clothes line, hung just the evening before.* She was playing, *"princess bride"*, and having a wonderful time of it from the look of my once white sheet.

Ah...thats what you get when you turn around and clean up after breakfast, **shooing the kids outside without direction! If you don't direct their energy, they will find something, on their own.**

So, **I asked the Lord for what I was beginning to suspect was a myth:**
A clean home,

    a manicured yard,

        well-behaved kids, and

            all laundry done -- **all in one day.**

Then I added, *"And, Lord, can I have a place to "create"--and it be just mine?*

    A garden or perhaps an art studio?"

When you ask for the moon, you might as well just go for it! Right?

FAST FORWARD 30 YEARS.

I was walking up my driveway looking at my yard and garden...thanking the Lord for all that he had given me. It was a beautiful day, blue sky...dewy from the rain the day before. Because of the rain, *I had spent my time inside cleaning and doing the laundry so...it was all done.*

I was feeling good and happy! My husband had poked his head out of the window and asked me, *"What do you have planned to do today? Everything is done. Why don't you go out and spend some time in your studio?"*

My husband (wonderful man) **had an art studio built for me for Christmas** and **it was finally completed at the end of April**. (That's what happens when you build in the winter, It takes longer because of rain, mud, lightening, freezing etc.)

THEN IT HIT ME!

The Lord reminded me of that request born of frustration and self-pity, so very long ago.
EVERYTHING I HAD ASKED FOR, HE HAD GIVEN IT IN HUGE PORTIONS!

My garden is large with high walls and raised beds for easy access and gravel paths around them—*but, it's not just that*--**The Lord has blessed my garden and it produces more than I ever expected, allowing us to have enough for us but also to share with all our neighbors and family.**

It has a large wrought Iron door for a gate, and everywhere there isn't vegetables, are flowers.
I LOVE IT! And I thank The Lord every day that I'm in it.

Our new house has a laundry room! *We didn't have one when the girls were little!*
We had to go to the laundromat or [later], the back porch, or garage.
It's amazing what easy access will do for a housewife! **THE LORD KNEW!**

The Art studio--More than a closet or converted bedroom--Someplace to put all my craft, fabric, sewing machines, easels for painting, etc.--all in one place and not have to put it away every night--Squirreling it all away, under beds and in closets--But **NOW,** all in one place! **WHAT A CONCEPT!**

Now remember...I had made this request **before** "She Sheds", or art studios became popular.
I just wanted a place to put it all together in one place. **AND NOW I HAVE IT!**
A beautiful 18 X 18 Room--complete with glass doors across the front for maximum light, beautiful bead board walls, complete with heat and air conditioning.
When the Lord answers prayer, he does it in a complete and perfect way.

You see, children get dirty and so does their clothes. As long as we have homes and choose to live clean, *there will be cleaning to do.* **Thats ok!** **THAT'S LIFE!**

I have always been grateful that I had a home to clean! **SOME DON'T!**

In those many years past, I wouldn't have been able to spend time in a garden, or art studio. **I worked!** Not just at home, but I also had a full-time job and I had children and a husband, and **that is where I needed to spend my energy and time.**

Not being selfish...shut in a studio creating or, pruning and picking in a garden. <u>I would have felt guilty.</u> **But 'everything in its season', and only the Lord knows when that is.**

I'm grateful that HE heard my Prayer...*pondered it,* put HIS INFINITE KNOWLEDGE *into play,* and **added my request** to HIS VERY LONG LIST OF THINGS TO ACCOMPLISH.

DOES IT ALL MATTER IN THE BIG PICTURE?

I would think No--<u>But it does</u>, *because if he listens to the little trivial stuff that we as the teeming mass of humanity tend to pour out, then we really have his attention about the stuff that really matters!*

THE LORD ALWAYS KEEPS HIS WORD!

And this simple daughter is humbled and forever grateful
THAT THE MASTER OF THE UNIVERSE,
took HIS Time to Listen, then Answer my Prayer with perfect timing.

THANK YOU LORD FOR ANSWERING MY PRAYER!

Chapter 25

THE POWER OF PRAYER!

Written by: **JULIE DARNELL**

FIRST I NEED TO SET THE STAGE AND GIVE YOU SOME BACK HISTORY.

My husband started having some health issues around the time he turned 70.

Up until that time he was never in the hospital for anything. A hardworking, very healthy, Blessed Man who took care of himself.

When he started having some issues and had to be put under anesthesia…

…ALL BETS WERE OFF!

Usually, **two to three hours after he came back from recovery,**

he turned into a real-life Hulk Hogan with hospital psychosis and extreme paranoia.

He was very fit and strong for his age so…

*…when this set in, it was pure havoc—***to put it lightly***.

Thrown in was his aged-onset-dementia, <u>*which made it even worse*</u>.

ONE PARTICULAR NIGHT WE WERE IN THE HOSPITAL …

…not even coming off the anesthesia, but were there for pneumonia this time.
As the sun goes down the 'Sundowner Syndrome' is real and starts.

Just like a switch had been turned on, or off --however, you want to look at it. With the Sundowners and the "hospital psychosis", *things were looking pretty grim.* **HE TURNED INTO THE HULK** in a *matter of minutes!* <u>At least 5 nurses</u>, male and female, were trying to calm and contain him.

<u>**He was strong, scared, confused and out of his mind**</u>.

It took 5 to contain him. When I say <u>contain</u>, *all they were able to do…*

<u>WAS KEEP HIM FROM JUMPING OUT OF THE BED.</u>

THIS ALL HAPPENED ON A WEDNESDAY NIGHT.

I knew the Choir at my church, was having practice.

I sent a text to the Preacher and asked him to pray. I told him what was happening. If you've never seen anyone in this 'mindset', consider yourself 'Blessed', because *it's one of the scariest, heartbreaking situations you can witness--and it can take days to pass.* <u>He had taken the Nurse's thermometer machine from her, and he thought it was a bomb and threatened to throw it</u>.

He was so afraid.

Honestly, <u>so were we</u>.

I had asked the Pastor to pray for him to calm down.

After I did that, they moved us to another room *<u>to keep us from the other patients,</u>* because things were loud and scary.

Minutes after we got to the room and I had reached out for prayer, *<u>a calm came over the room.</u>*

He looked over and handed the Nurse her thermometer machine back.
<u>The room was silent</u>.

We all looked at each other trying to figure out what just happened.

I TOLD THIS STORY TO SOMEONE WHO WAS AT CHOIR PRACTICE.
She told me when I sent the text to the Pastor,
<u>they stopped Choir practice and they all prayed immediately for him.</u>
He calmed down! <u>The peace that they prayed for him, came into that room.</u>
I've never felt or seen anything like what happened in that room that night.
<u>They did not give him anything medicinally. They weren't able to.</u>

This was God. Thank you Jesus.

Chapter 26

PEACE THROUGH 'HIS' PROTECTION!

Written by: **SALLY SANDERS FREE**

IN MY LIFE I HAVE WITNESSED MANY MIRACLES!

When I was one & half, my dad was in the car, ***headed to the store for my mom.***

<u>*She forgot to put an item on the list so she ran outside to tell my dad*</u>.

She left the sliding glass doors open, and I **followed** her out to the car.

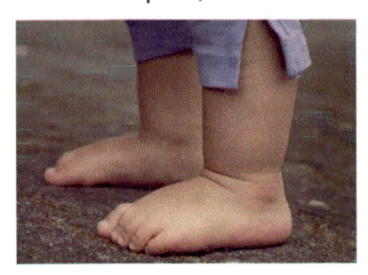

<u>*She had no clue I ran out with her, and was behind the car*</u>.

My dad didn't see me, either. **As he backed up the car, he ran over me!**

After spending a week in the hospital, running test –

<u>no broken bones or internal injuries.</u>

<u>Just a few cuts and bruises.</u>

FAST FORWARD

AFTER I MARRIED AND HAD CHILDREN,
MY DAUGHTER AND I SURVIVED A PLANE CRASH!

My employer was a landscaping company. Part of my responsibilities was to '<u>fly-over</u>' sod-farms, <u>to determine if the sod met the needs of our potential clients</u>.

My boss would send me on 'day-trips', to investigate various properties.

On this particular trip, my daughter, [13 years old], **begged to go with me** and <u>I had given in</u> and let her tag along.

<u>We boarded a private jet at McCollum Airport.</u>

The plane carried 2 pilots & 8 passengers.

We were flying back from South Georgia after looking at a sod farm.

Suddenly, we were aware that something was wrong!

The men on the plane were panicking!
I will never forget all the men on the plane calling their wives and crying,

saying we were going to die.

To my surprise, I sat there with such calmness and told Christian **we were going to be okay**.

The problem was, that one side of the landing gear was stuck.

First, trying to 'unstick' the gear with the various controls in the cockpit…didn't work!

One of the pilots had an idea of how to correct the problem.
    The pilot told us his plan.
Because he had just refueled the plane while we were out looking at the farm on golf carts, [which meant we had enough fuel to accomplish this maneuver],

he was going to try and do a quick touchdown on the ground. His hope was that the landing gear would pop up.

But, again—**THAT DIDN'T WORK!**

His next plan was to ride around and dump the fuel…
    …to assist in a 'safer' emergency landing.
Our pilot, who I know was guided by the hands of God, did a phenomenal job.
He let us know what to expect when we landed, and, said he had called in the Calvary.
(fire trucks, police, & ambulances).

WE FINALLY DUMPED ALL THE FUEL.

He then told us to get in position for a rough landing.

I sat there hugging and reassuring Christian…
that **God had us and that we were going to be okay.**
We hit the runway—
the plane 'bellyflopped' and rolled–
as we slid down the runway—
breaking the wing off and flipping us up on our side.
When the plane finally stopped, the pilot instructed us to stay in our seat…
until they cleared the aisle and opened the emergency hatch.

The men went running out of that plane in panic in front of me and Christian.
--crying like this was the end for them--

As we got out of the plane, I called my husband, Chris, and told him what had happened to us, and that we were fine. **He about had a heart attack after hearing this!**

Chris said, *"God had to be on our side today."*
"Yes," I said, *"God took care of us and sent my two Guardian Angels,*
(my momma & daddy), *to let me know that we were going to be okay."*

That is why I had felt such peace while going through such a horrific experience. Peace came over me when I heard my parents' voices in my head, and felt their presence.

We had no injuries day! All thanks goes to The Good Lord Above!

Fear not [there is nothing to fear], for I am with you; do not look around you in terror *and* be dismayed, for I am your God. I will strengthen *and* harden you to difficulties, yes, I will help you; yes, I will hold you up *and* retain you with My [victorious] right hand of rightness *and* justice. Isaiah 41:10 -- Amplified Bible, Classic Edition

I HAVE HAD MANY LIFE CHANGING MOMENTS IN MY LIFE...

...**the birth of my children,** the death of my parents/ & three siblings,

fifteen surgeries in my life, **multiple car accidents that I survived,**

and **a husband with myasthenia gravis,**
a rare disease that effects the muscles and nerves in his body.

Through all my trials and blessings here on earth, God has been with me through them all!

He has never forsaken me!

I call on him and he always sees me through and always gives me strength to carry on.

I know in my heart that God has always put a protection shield around me.

For I the Lord your God hold your right hand; I am the Lord, Who says to you, Fear not; I will help you!
Isaiah 41:13 = Amplified Bible, Classic Edition

Only God knows how my or your story will end!
He knows what is going to happen to me before I do.

He also knows what sins that I (or you) will commit, before we do!

One of Gods greatest gifts to us, is **He is a Forgiving God!** My faith in God *gives me strength, hope, peace, and love.* I do not know what tomorrow holds for me and my family, **but God knows!**
I JUST KNOW I WILL CLING TO MY FAITH IN THE GOOD LORD, AND ENJOY THE JOURNEY ALL THE WAY TO THE END!

...constantly bearing in mind your work of faith and labor of love and steadfastness of hope in our Lord Jesus Christ in the presence of our God and Father,,, 1 Thessalonians 1:3

...But now faith, hope, love, abide these three; but the greatest of these... 1 Corinthians 13:13

...And Jesus *answered saying to them, "Have faith in God"... Mark 11:22

Chapter 27

GOD'S WORD-*PROMISES*-GOD'S PRESENCE!

Written by: LORNA FERRIS JOSEPH

A PRICELESS GIFT

One beautiful day back in my childhood, **my father (Fred) brought home a book**
<u>**that would change my life forever.**</u>

As he gathered us together to share the book we looked on with excitement because in those days **most households in Antigua had few.** *This book became a family treasure* and one that would bring me **peace, joy, comfort, wisdom and knowledge.**

That day, Pappy unveiled a copy of the **Holy Bible**.

He encouraged us all to read it.

As children, the Bible was a book from which

we had learned memory verses in Sunday school,

but <u>never had one to hold and call our very own</u>.

Excited and ready to delve into this precious book (that would soon be the foundation of my life) was not easy.

At the beginning of my quest...

...**reading and understanding** the Bible **was very challenging** since **my education ended at Fourteen years old.** In the face of this challenge, *I pressed on for I knew there was*

something miraculous within these pages

that would help me to navigate through the rest of my life.

It was more than challenging as I kept trying to read and understand the word of God.

Very determined, this day before reading,
I uttered a simple, but powerful prayer.

I asked God to ***teach me His word and give me the understanding*** thereof.

HE DID!

Day by day, <u>as I continued to read</u> ...it was as if God himself was reading to me.

<u>**MY GOD IS REAL AND ALWAYS READY TO AID US AND CARRY US ON LIFE'S JOURNEY.**</u>

Through the reading of the scriptures during my adolescence,

I learned how to fully trust in the Lord with my heart, body and soul.

Surrendering all my needs (as life would continue to bring more challenges than I could imagine),

but I am *forever* grateful for that day my father *gave us that wonderful gift.*

A PRICELESS SAVIOR

It is a blessing to be saved and know that I have a friend in Jesus.

I love the Christian life and with assurance I can boast of my Savior and all He has done for me.

Praying, focusing on God's Word and giving thanks has been the key through life's difficult journey. Prayer is an integral part of my journey.

It is where I have gained strength to make it through.
Although I have great stories of *challenges and disappointments,*

moments of that beautiful day my dad gave us the Bible

will shine through and encourage my heart.

So let us shake the dust off our Bibles and go deeper in His word and draw closer to Him. Intimacy with Christ Jesus is how I have made it through life's hardships and still has the ability to sing joyously, dance and praise Him.

Let Him in and I guarantee you will never regret it.

It is my delight to study God's word, to sing out my praise to God and dance before Him. I love to pray to the One Eternal God. He is my present help (Psalm 46:1) and He knows my every care:

"God is our refuge and strength, a very present help in trouble." [KJV]

A PRICELESS HEALER

Throughout my life, I had five different surgeries. Each time I prayed and asked God to take over my situation and do what only He can do.
Before my first surgery in 1984 in Puerto Rico, I prayed and asked God to disappoint the doctor and not let him find what he is looking for.

After my surgery, my answer came exactly the way I asked Him.
The first words out of my doctor's mouth were,

"Lorna, I am disappointed. I did not find what I was looking for."

God put His hand in my situation. I went home to Antigua with a testimony. In Forty-Five years, I never had that problem again.

Praise and thanks be to God!

Hebrews 10:35 – "Cast not away therefore your confidence, which hath great recompence of reward." [KJV]

A PRICELESS COMFORTER

Another time while the anesthesia was setting in for surgery, I had a struggling in my spirit.

It seemed like I was tossing and turning.

Then I heard His still, soft voice saying, "Relax, Relax."

I settled down and relaxed.

When I came through everything was alright.

PRAISE HIS NAME! He came through for me! I heard the voice of God again.

"...but we glory in tribulations also: knowing that tribulation worketh patience; And patience, experience; and experience, hope: And hope maketh not ashamed..." (Romans 5:3-5) [KJV].

Persistence brings results. PRAISE ALMIGHTY GOD! Walk in obedience.

My mother (Daisy) always told us that obedience is the key to all that is required of mankind by God. I am grateful for her words because obedience has brought me hope in Christ without shame.

A PRICELESS PROMISE KEEPER

My most recent surgery came on me suddenly. I was scheduled for major surgery on May 29th, 2024. After completing my pre-surgery prep the night before, I started talking with God.

My prayer was, *"Here I am Lord another time. I am reminiscing and going back to 1984. You brought me out (of surgery) safely. I know You have never done a case that You cannot do again. Father, put Your righteous right hand in my situation and do what only You can do.*

Take over. You are the Great Physician*!"*

Praise God, I went off to sleep and rested well!

Finally, the day of my surgery was here. When I arrived at the hospital…

…everything went smoothly and quickly with my pre-opt preparation.

I waited patiently with my family to be taken to the operating room since my surgeon was delayed by a previous surgery.

A PRICELESS TOUCH

Then word came. *It was time and I was taken into surgery.*

While the anesthesia was taking effect,

I saw only the lower portion of a forearm down to just below the wrist (not the hand). The hand appeared to be in my side. This must be the hand of God.

He put His Righteous Hand into my right side, just as I prayed.

As I began to slowly awake out of the anesthesia, my family and nurses heard me say,

"HE TOUCHED ME! HE TOUCHED ME!"

They all asked, "Who touched you?" My response was, "Jesus touched me!"

_____

My recovery has been a good journey. All my test results have been great.

I experienced God's Healing Touch again!

ALL GLORY AND PRAISE TO GOD FOR HE IS FAITHFUL!

Many times I have shared my life stories about my surgeries. Each surgery has its own unique story, but they all have one thing in common—

I sought the Lord. He heard and answered my prayers each time.

My Jesus healed me and left my doctors in awe of my recovery.

Having the Greatest Physician as the lead doctor on my case has helped me to go through these difficulties so many times in my life.

Over the years, *I have thanked God for the day—*

my Pappy brought home our family Bible.

My gratitude to God for His continuous teaching of His word—

with understanding will go on forever.

Chapter 28

'SOME THROUGH THE FIRE'!

Written by: TAMMIE POWELL

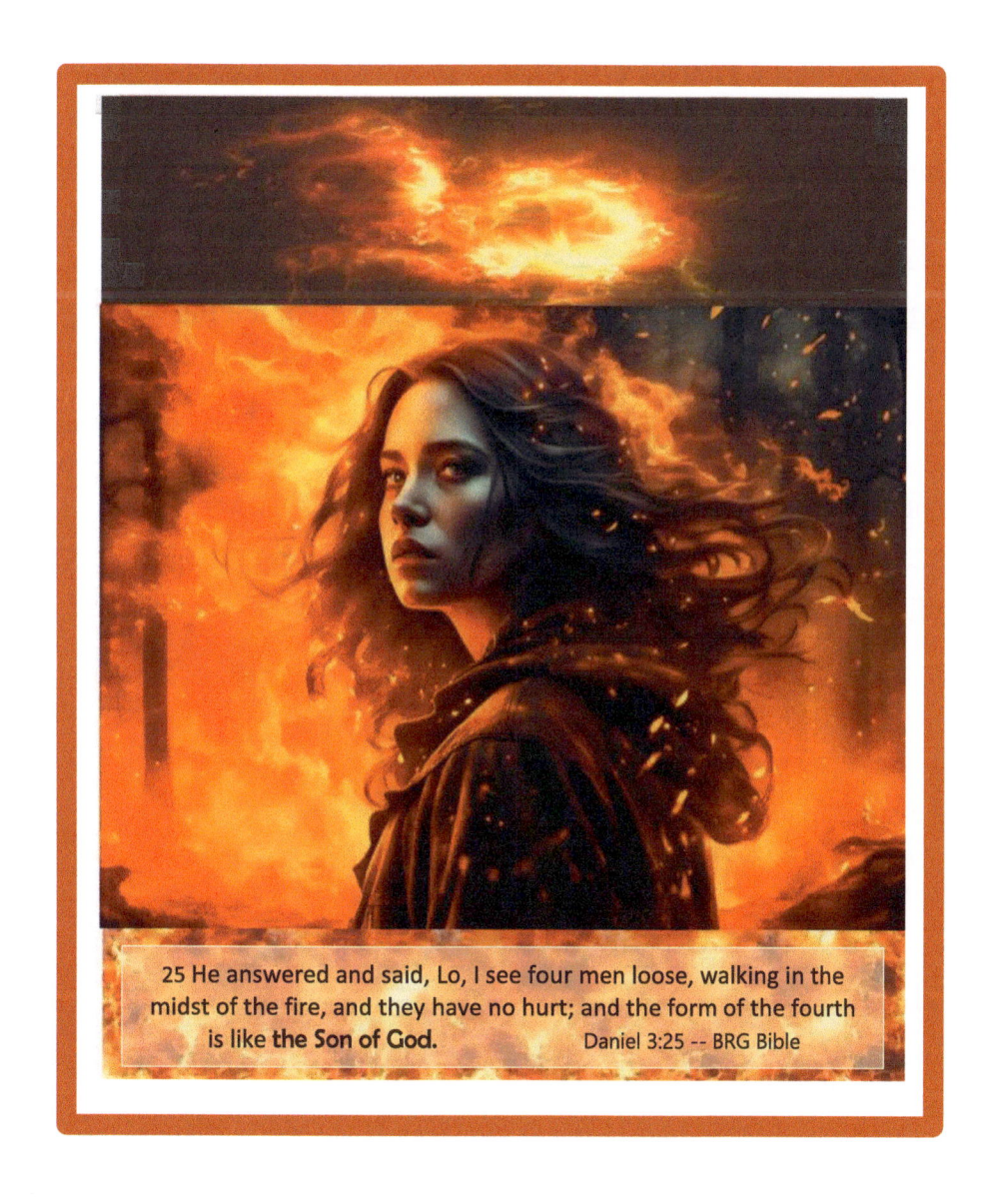

> 25 He answered and said, Lo, I see four men loose, walking in the midst of the fire, and they have no hurt; and the form of the fourth is like **the Son of God.** Daniel 3:25 -- BRG Bible

November 8th, 2018, was a Thursday like no other in our family history.

Oddly enough, it started like every other work day, get up, get ready, off to work.

I worked at the Department of Employment and Social Services, in the town of Oroville, a 20-minute drive from my house at 3179 Goa-way, Paradise, California. My regular route was to head south down Neal Road to highway 99, make a left onto the highway, then straight to Oroville.

I started work at 7:30 am, but liked to arrive early to open everything up and get rolling. My supervisor came in around 8 am with the other employees. **My office was an interior office** with no windows, so she asked me to come look at something.

IT WAS THE SKY! The back of our building faced **Table Mountain** and the Highway 70 northern corridor to Lake Oroville. You could clearly see **a cloud** with a **red and gold halo on top,** *the wind was moving it* towards **Lower Paradise**, in the **Lime Saddle Area**.

My heart sank! We had lived with so many fires in the past, but this was different—
--no black smoke, just hot white, red and gold.

I thought, *"It must have just started!"* We ran inside to check our computers. Being county personal, we were the "**boots on the ground**"! Social services opens the evacuation centers prior to any state agency's arrival, like **FEMA**.

I opened up the link to CDF, and their local incident reports. Nothing but a brief clip about a small fire up Hwy 70 by Pulga. They were calling it **"The Camp Fire"**, at this time.

I looked around at my class of employees (I was a Trainer for Social Services). I called home. No one answered! *My Boss and I exchanged a long look*. She asked me if I thought we were ok there at our offices. I said, "**only if the wind does not change**".

I called home again, no answer. All this time she was watching me. She was a city girl, and trusted my instincts (they had saved us before), I stated, "*I need to leave!*" At the same time, she stated, "*You need to leave.*"

I had already turned off my computer—picked up my purse—heading for the door. I knew this was different. I wasn't sure how—just knew it was.

> What I haven't mentioned was that my Mother-in-Law lived with my husband and me. Her name is Ione, but we call her GG, short for Great Grandmother. She is nearly deaf, and wouldn't hear the sheriff's department or Fire department if they came calling. She is the one I was trying to call. If she was close to the phone she might hear it—I tried again from my cell in the car—no answer, and my anxiety ratcheted up considerably.

I HIT THE HWY 70 ON-RAMP GOING 70 MPH!

I pulled up behind a CHP, who was looking in his rear view at me. I figured he could follow me home to ticket me if he wanted to. But I figured he had bigger problems.

In my rearview mirror, I saw Sheriff Department Cruisers coming in fast, **pulled over** into the right lane without slowing. **The three cars** ...wn the highway--all of us keeping pace. The CHP **took the** ..., but spun around on the ramp.

I then realized he was closing the road!

My heart was pounding! I might not make it in time! *They might have already closed the road.*
I accelerated! **The Sheriff's cruiser passed me. It was a familiar one. One who shared the daily commute with me and knew my car.**

He shook his finger at me as he passed.
I followed him. **We were doing around 90 mph.**

I wanted to go faster but didn't dare. As I look back—there were no cars on the road!

All I could see, once we rounded the corner from Hwy 70, was the **massive fire cloud** arcing across the sky. It now filled the horizon from Hwy 70 to Skyway. I was driving too fast to call home, again.

I had to shake myself and steady myself for what was to come.

I was terrified for GG and my family.

When I finally made it to the Neal Road turn off of Hwy 99, the Sheriff's cruiser was in front of me. But as *he spun the cruiser around*, I hit the gas and sped up the hill past him.
I saw in my rearview mirror that he closed the road behind me—blocking the road with his cruiser.

I was almost home. **Please—please—please, God—let me get there in time!**
The sky was getting dark. I knew it was houses burning!
Only houses have totally black smoke.
It wasn't the terribly beautiful white hot, red and gold anymore—
  but something much more sinister, **ash and black.**

I pulled my car into our circle drive, for an easy escape, and literally ran to the door.

111

THERE WAS GG, SITTING TWO FEET FROM THE TV,

clutching the phone, and the remote. **She was terrified!**
I tried to call my husband, who answered halfway through the first ring, saying, "Get mom and get out. I am stuck in town and its insane! A complete juggernaut of crazy panicked people— all trying to evacuate. **Don't wait for me!"**

He said he would find a way to go to our daughter's house in Durham.

At that time, our youngest daughter called. she asked If I was home.

I said, "Yes, I'm here now. Where are you? Why are you running?"

She said, she had to leave her car in a parking lot—*that the town was on fire*—not just a building, *but the whole place!* She stated that she was running down skyway, pulling her daughter behind her and said that *cars were burning in the road*. I told her to meet us at her sister's house and not to worry about us—to **just get out safe.**

She said **she could see her husband** in his truck in the distance—**her son was waving** his arms out the window trying to get her attention.

I could breathe! Her husband would die before letting anything happen to her. *I had not realized that I had been holding myself rigid with fear for my family.* I was completely terrified for her.

GG and I went into the living room (the power was off). My husband came *crashing in the door,* with flashlights blazing, *covered in ashes,* **OUR HERO!** He said that we have to go now--that *there is ash with hot embers landing in the yard*. GG said she could drive her car, so, my husband simply gave her the key and stated. *"Stay right behind me, okay?"*

So we started out our little lane, *only to realize that our single lane Neal road* was **an insane highway!** We waited for some time just trying to get onto the road.

No one would let us on!

It was bumper to bumper—with only inches between cars.

As we waited, **large embers were landing all around and on us** and **small flames were starting to burn in the grass in the fields,** alongside the road. After some time, someone in a very large black truck, *stopped the traffic* by pulling his truck across the road so we could pull on.
I am so very grateful for that person!! God bless them whomever they are.

The traffic was barely moving—you could almost walk faster! Suddenly, a lot of cars started passing on the left-hand side—they were driving very fast, **with smoking tires!**

I LOOKED INTO MY REARVIEW MIRROR AND MY HEART SANK—

--I saw flames in the distance—*that's why they had panicked*. Emergency crews in CDF and Sheriff Vehicles started coming passing fast, and the people that had tried to escape the flames by going down the left side of the road were pushed off the road—some in the ditch—others trying to get back on the road. **IT WAS CHAOS!**

As I watched the fire advance behind me, I looked over the ravine back toward my home and saw it burning—**took a picture**—and *started crying*.

[Another home gone due to a fire, you see…we had also lost a home to fire in December, 1999, and went through the fire in 2006, when all the homes but ours burnt around us. You see, my husband and his brother stayed at the house in 2006, fighting the fire even after the fire crews had given up, but they had saved it. Not this time!]

It took us 4 hours to drive what usually takes 15 minutes! Everyone's vehicles were bumper to bumper. **Tempers were high** and the anxiety just kept going up. Everyone could see the fire in the distance—around the landfill and crossing to skyway. We watched fist-fights—and fender benders—guns being pulled and pointed—**witnessed true grace** and conversely, **pure selfishness**. It was an insane spectacle of human nature. I thought,

"how does a community come back from this"—"how, when there is nothing to return to"!

We finally arrived at our daughter's house in Durham. *We called as many family members as we could, networking to be sure we were all present and accounted for*. The Powell family was 4 generations deep and, due to the fire, flung far and wide—
no longer in the same community where we all grew up.

We hugged, cried and prayed for the family members that couldn't be reached by phone.

From this point forward, I started shaking inside. It didn't stop for about 2 years. Before the fire, I was 130 pounds. By the time a year rolled around, I was 114 pounds, which is the weight I stayed at until this fall, October 2021 [I'm 5 ft 7in,]. The doctor told me I was too thin for my height. I have an appetite—just nervous all the time. I jump easily at the slightest sound. GG is far worse. All of 95 pounds and 5 feet, 1 in, she was so jumpy we would have to peel her off the ceiling—no matter how we announce ourselves.

The rest is kind of a blur. We lived with our daughter Breanna, in Durham, with her two sons and wonderful husband (not one complaint the entire time). It is a 3 bedroom, 2 bath house. GG slept in our grandson's room on his twin bed with baseballs on the head board.

We purchased a camper in Roseville, parked it in their driveway, and slept in that. We had heat, but no bathroom. So we had to run inside to the bathroom—in the winter at night is no fun—but we were grateful, **we had our lives**.

It was an impossible situation!

There were no apartments, houses, duplexes or any housing available within a 2-hour drive of our work. Houses to purchase went up daily by the thousands. People were asking one hundred thousand dollars more than the asking price and getting it.

I started back to work after a week, which was a mistake. One third of the employees had lived in paradise. It took a huge toll on all the departments. **Social Services was slammed with applications for aid**, as well as running the FEMA/ Fire relief centers. Let me tell you, it's very difficult to get over a catastrophic event in your life, if every day you relive it through all the people you are trying to help. **Because it's your job, there was no escape.**

Social Services offered counseling, **which I took advantage of.** They started with large groups in a circle, *to share their experiences,* **which always ended in tears for everyone. I stopped going!** *It was way too hard to return to work after that raw exposure.*

You see, the free counseling was done during the work day! Hard to shake it off and be a productive employee, after that.

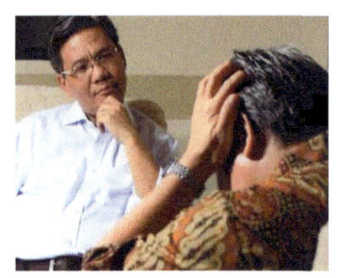

No amount of time seems to heal the decision that was forced upon us.

OUR COMMUNITY STRUGGLES THROUGH THE MAGNITUDE OF TRAGEDIES!

The paperwork for our burned proprieties from the county was overwhelming—**they were overwhelmed as well, and were learning as they went. So information from them was always changing, which kept you always in a tail spin!**

There was always a new form that had to be filed;

new fees to be paid;

new hoops to be jumped through.

It was government bureaucracy at its worst. I can only hope that this was put to good use and things worked out for the future, I hope they never need it again.

We thought that we would be able to live in our travel trailers on our property while we re-built. The county said no! The area must be cleared. But there were no available spaces to rent. **Another impossible situation.** You see,

114

THE EVACUATION WAS COMPLETE, BUT THE HITS JUST KEPT COMING.

Regrouping is difficult at best, but our area had already been hit by the fires in Redding, California. **Our available housing had been filled by those poor people**.

Now there was none for the Camp Fire Victims.

People were living in tents at Walmart.

Purchasing options were almost non-existent!

You couldn't buy a suitcase, or plastic tub--even underwear.

Our lives mainly consisted of work, home, paperwork, look for housing.

It was pretty much in that order.

On a day in early February, our son in law, Wayne, came to me one day and asked if I would be interested in **an apartment that might be available for rent**. *He knew someone who was moving to Redding for work, but had signed a two-year lease at his apartment complex.* **He was looking for someone to assume his lease**. We jumped up at the same time. **Yes! We could do that!**

We got the apartment in March.

It was wonderful having private space--<u>our own bathroom</u>!

GG was out of our grandson's bed.

It was wonderful! We were very grateful.

Unforeseen Health Consequences

That spring my husband Tod came down with a respiratory infection, he was treated and sent home. Since then, he has had pneumonia twice and is on an inhaler.

[He is also being seen by a respiratory specialist.]

When asked if he was a smoker, they are surprised to find out that he never smoked. **They stated that he probably has** smoke damage to his lungs due to his prolonged time in Paradise while trying to evacuate while breathing the black smoke of burning homes.

[He is still receiving a prescribed inhaler for his breathing.]

OUR NEW BEGINNING!
The summer of July, 2019, we visited our daughters in Georgia.

While there, we went on a country drive. It was beautiful, green and lush—just like Paradise used to be—trees were everywhere! We had forgotten what it felt like to be among the trees. You see I was born in Greenville, California, which sadly, also burned to the ground last year. I'm a mountain girl! One that loves trees. I really didn't want to leave California. But, because we loved the area in Georgia, my husband looked at a house in Woodstock—put in an offer, and 15 days later we were home owners in Georgia.

GOD'S GRACE BROUGHT US THROUGH IT ALL!

We are unbelievably grateful for our lives, and the lives of our family members.
Our family has learned that Love keeps us — not things!

Things can be replaced, not people, not relationships!

Through it all, we discovered that the **"Family Unit"**, is expressly created by God, *for our betterment.*

When I say Family, **I mean relatives, loved ones, friends, the people we surround ourselves with.**

We are stronger, fight harder, love more deeply,
when we have something or someone to fight for,
and that they would in turn do the same for us.

Isn't that what God wants us to do? **Take care of each other?** Love one another?

So...If you reader, don't have a family, don't worry! Get one—join a Church, Bible study, Choir, or charity group. *Surround yourself with people who Love the Lord.*
They encourage you! You can in turn, be there for them.

As long as God, Jesus and Love are the focus, you are on the right track!

KEEP GOING!

Chapter 29

'WHAT YOU THINK…YOU ARE'!

Written by: CAROL McGINNIS YEJE

OUR FAITH IS DETERMINED BY WHAT WE REALLY THINK!

When Martha said,

"...*whatsoever thou wilt ask of God, God Will Give It thee*...",

she really THOUGHT she meant every word. [John 11:22]

But then when Jesus tells her,

"...*Thy brother shall rise again*...",

she 'automatically' THOUGHT He meant in the "...*resurrection at the last day*". [John 11:23-24]

Martha had just said that she knew God would do anything that Jesus asked. Then, with the same tongue, she showed what she THOUGHT was 'not' what she 'SAID'.

Has God ever told you to do something by faith...

 ...I mean *totally* by faith...

 ...and HE assured you that 'something' was surely going to come to pass?

 But, as time 'rocked-on', for you to 'continue' to believe that 'something'—

He had to tell you AGAIN...

...before it 'actually' took 'hold' and made you take 'action on your faith'.

What happened was that **God had to reveal to you,**

your true-self...

...what you 'thought' you were...you 'weren't'.

We can testify and sing… "Oh, how I love Jesus" …or shout to the 'house-tops'…

"Lord, I'll go!" And, maybe, that's what we THOUGHT, we 'thought'.

But The Lord will send a **90-foot wave crashing by** *to reveal to us* **what we really THOUGHT**…

not *what we've been telling everybody we 'thought'.*

And, then, **when the 'real thoughts' come out,**
 we realize what we really ARE.

If you can't shout in the heat of battle,
don't think you've got God fooled one bit *when you shout in peacetime.*

And, *you'll even let those around you see that* **your 'armor' is slipping,** *if you're not really careful.*

Even when Jesus explained to Martha—
 "…I AM that Resurrection and The Life…Believest thou this?",
she still responded with— *"I believe that Thou Art 'The Christ'…*
 The Son of God…which should come into the world." [John 11:26-27]

You may have acknowledged that Jesus Christ is 'The Savior Of The World'.
You may have accepted Him as your Personal Savior and are truly 'Born Again'.

But—WHO DO YOU 'REALLY' THINK JESUS IS?

What Jesus was trying to get across to Martha was that
He HAD ALL POWER.

Do you THINK Jesus has 'ALL' power?

You do know that the 'seat' of your heart is your mind!

"...as he thinketh in his heart, so is he..."; [Proverbs 23:7]

...the *"...heart is deceitful above all things..."*; [Jeremiah 17:9]

"...with the heart man believeth." [Romans 10:10]

Some definitions of 'think', are: 'to form or conceive in the mind';

'to hold as an opinion'; 'to reflect upon the matter in question'; <u>'TO BELIEVE'</u>.

The dictionary says that the heart is *'...the seat of life, thought, or emotion'*.

So, you see...it all boils down to the fact that <u>Martha did **NOT** BELIEVE</u>,

<u>with all her 'being'</u>,

<u>that Jesus had 'ALL POWER'!</u>

If we only MEANT what we SAID we BELIEVE,

WHAT GREAT WORKS FOR GOD *we could do 'through' Jesus,*

<u>GUIDED BY THE HOLY SPIRIT</u> !

| **HEAVENLY FATHER!** Please help us to 'truly believe' in the Power and Authority of the Name and Divinity of Jesus, our Savior! | | **DEAR JESUS!** Please help us to 'grow stronger in Faith'— acknowledging You as OUR SAVIOR... making YOU, LORD OF OUR LIVES! |